SECRETS *of*
SUCCESSFUL
NEGOTIATING
W*for*OMEN

*From Landing a Big Account to Buying the Car of
Your Dreams and Everything in Between*

WENDY KELLER

CASTLE BOOKS

This edition published in 2005 by
CASTLE BOOKS ®
A division of Book Sales, Inc.
114 Northfield Avenue
Edison, NJ 08837

This edition published by arrangement with
Career Press
3 Tice Road
Franklin Lakes, NJ 07417

Secrets of Successful Negotiating for Women © 2004 Wendy Keller.
Original English language edition published by Career Press

Secrets of Successful Negotiating for Women
Edited and Typeset by KATIE HENCHES

Library of Congress Cataloging-in-Publication Data

Keller, Wendy, 1964-
Secrets of successful negotiating for women : from landing a big account to
buying the car of your dreams and everything in between / by Wendy
Keller.
p. cm.
        Includes bibliographical references and index.
        1.   Negotiation in business. 2. Businesswomen. 3. Women.
        I. Title.

HD58.6.K447 2004   2004045852
158'.5—dc22

ISBN-13: 978-0-7858-2106-9
ISBN-10: 0-7858-2106-6

Printed in the United States of America

Dedication

To women everywhere,
who know there is a better way.

And to my daughter Sophia,
and all our daughters:
May you create harmony and abundance
in your lives always.

Acknowledgments

There are always dozens of people behind any successful book, and thousands of people who have crossed the author's path. These thousands seep into our minds and inspire the books we will eventually write. Thank you to the thousands, but the dozens can be named most easily.

I'd like to thank my publisher Ron Fry, whose business savvy is legendary in the publishing industry and whose gruff exterior belies a kind heart. I'd also like to give much gratitude to my editors Michael Lewis and Michael Pye, clever men with quick minds, who leave authors alone between contract and delivery date. (The best sort of editors to have, I assure you!) Special thanks to Kate Henches, whose copy editing skills cut through my fuzzy memories of the *Chicago Manual of Style* like a hot knife through low-fat margarine.

Sincere and special thanks to the women you'll meet in these pages. Thank you for sharing your insights with us all.

To my mentors and friends, whose wisdom and examples guide and inspire me: His Holiness the Dalai Lama, don Miguel Ruiz, Ernestine Fischer, Marc Allen, Mark Victor Hansen, Dr. Jack Lin, George Silverman, Garrett Keller, Greg Stein, Ellae Elinwood, and Dr. Jayne Gardner.

To those no longer living but whose words change lives daily and guide mine always including Napoleon Hill, Andrew Carnegie, Henry Clay Frick, JP Morgan, Benjamin Franklin, Mary Wollstonecraft, Leonardo da Vinci, Henry VIII, Victoria Holt, Barbara Cartland, Swifty Lazear, Alexander Rudolph, Bertha Louisa Elsa Holsa Swanson, Jeremy Winston Zhorne, Amelia Louise Zhorne: Namaste. You are my guiding lights.

Finally, with much gratitude for her unfathomable patience while Mom wrote yet another book, the most precious person in my life, a bearer of wisdom and a pure spirit on this planet, I thank my daughter Sophia Rose.

Contents

The Seven Sisters of Negotiation Success

The First Principle:

We live in a world overflowing with abundance.

The Second Principle:

Negotiation is creating a situation in which both parties feel they got a fair deal.

The Third Principle:

Successful negotiation usually requires creativity.

The Fourth Principle:

Know what you want and what's possible.

The Fifth Principle:

Be prepared.

The Sixth Principle:

Bring and show your best and highest self.

The Seventh Principle:

Stand by your product, service, or word.

Introduction

Great negotiation skills are perhaps the most important tools you will use whether it be within your life, your family, your career, or your relationships. To be able to easily view the situation from three perspectives (yours, theirs, and the overall) will give you the invaluable ability to quickly determine a solution that's best for everyone.

As you study this book and practice the techniques described, you will liberate your mind from the focus of just one negotiation in which you may be currently involved, to seeing all of life as a negotiation. You will learn to employ your own natural graciousness without sacrificing your self or your rights. You will learn to manifest what you need out of a situation, or, worst case, have the courage and dignity to walk away if the deal just isn't going to meet your needs.

The book you hold contains priceless advice from smart women about all forms of negotiation. Its purpose is to help you wield your power as a woman so that every situation respects your own needs and boundaries as well as those of the other parties If you end your reading of this book with an improved sense of confidence in your ability to get what you want in the world in a fair, ethical, and elegant way, then you will have achieved the goal I set for my readers when writing.

In these pages, you'll learn from all sorts of women. I've interviewed a high-powered business executive, a gentle parenting expert, a professional negotiator, a fine arts dealer, and many other women with different jobs and roles in between. Most of them are just like you with issues and concerns precisely like yours. By collecting the tips from these, your unseen sisters, you will be given a chance to see how different women handle a variety of situations. Most importantly, you will be given new, fresh perspectives on how to best manage the negotiations you encounter.

In a perfect world, I could promise you that when you finish reading this book, the rest of your negotiations—from why your kid doesn't put dirty socks in the hamper to your next promotion to the great deal you could get on your next car—will go exactly as you want. Sorry. This book will only skew the odds dramatically in your favor. When it comes to dirty socks, well, your guess on how to negotiate with a kid is as good as mine.

We know that life doesn't always go just as we'd like. In the real world of rough and tumble, instant decisions and constant negotiations, the solid proven core skills you will learn here will give you the ability to smooth out the speed bumps on your path. I wish you all the best!

Wendy Keller
Malibu, California
May 2004

CHAPTER 1

Touching Your Inherent Power

"The only way to know love is to experience love, to have the courage to jump into the ocean of love, and perceive it in it's totality. Once you experience love, you can't find the words to explain what you feel, but you see love coming from everyone, from everything, from everywhere."
—don Miguel Ruiz, teacher,
The Voice of Knowledge

There is a higher standard for women, in life and in negotiation, than there is for the average male. We are the peacekeepers, the mothers, daughters, and wives. We are the ones who tend to value more harmonious relationships and fair trade. We can easily visualize the bigger picture without losing sight of the vision in front of us now.

Fully mature, evolved women approach the art and science of negotiation almost as a spiritual practice. To create a deal that leaves each party's needs fairly and rightfully fulfilled takes skill and deep wisdom, not a collection of party tricks or memorized phrases. To satisfy our own needs while playing our role in the larger scheme of the world takes dignity, strength, and clear-mindedness.

Every deal has a heart, a life of its own. The people involved often have the very quality of lives at stake. When you are negotiating for a new car, you love the vehicle—the power of the motor, the beauty of its exterior, its practicality, the price, or some other element that brings you joy. You believe owning this car will improve the quality of your life. You'll feel safer, faster, better, smarter, richer, more beautiful when you drive it.

The salesperson has his own love affair with that car. That love affair is entwined in the commission from the sale. The money he earns will help him pay his bills, keep his family fed, create a future, pay for his son's college tuition, help him keep his job.

The sales manager has numbers to make. She has to move a certain number of cars off the lot in order to keep her job. She has her own family to feed, her own bills to pay, her mother's in-home nursing to pay for. You don't know what she needs when you walk in.

The owner of the dealership, the manufacturer, all the people on the assembly line between the steel factory and the car in front of you all have responsibilities, dreams, and goals not too different from your own. Every one of us wants to feel good about our lives, feel proud of our work and the profit it brings. Everyone wants to pay her bills and feed her family and have some luxuries.

Buying a car isn't a mere transaction between you and the salesperson standing in front of you. It's you interacting with the lives of thousands of people. They need you every bit as much as you need them.

Commerce, trade, and negotiation are all part of a big wheel, a big cycle, a big place called "Earth." In 1972, professor Edward Lorenz presented a paper to his colleagues in which he wondered if a butterfly flapping its wings in one place could affect the storm patterns across the world. According to his model, it does. So ask yourself: *Does the deal you make on this one car really affect all those thousands of people?*

Yes.

Aren't you just one person, with just one little tiny deal to make, a deal that affects very little in the overall picture of life?

No.

Sometimes we forget.

"Our deepest fear is not that we are inadequate.
"Our deepest fear is that we are powerful beyond measure. It is our light, not our darkness that most frightens us.

"We ask ourselves, 'Who am I to be brilliant, gorgeous, talented, and fabulous?' Actually, who are we not to be?

"You are a child of God. Your playing small doesn't serve the world. There's nothing enlightened about shrinking so that other people won't feel insecure around you.

"You were born to make manifest the glory of God that is within you. It is not just in some of us. It's in every one.

"As we let our own light shine, we unconsciously give other people permission to do the same. As we are liberated from our own fear, our presence automatically liberates others."

—*A Return to Love: Reflections on the Principles of a Course on Miracles,*
by Marianne Williamson

Sometimes we forget, in the business of birthing, living, and dying, that every one of us is a component of the planet. That we have a noble purpose while we live: to play nice with others and to share our toys. The things our mothers taught us—the timeless, cross-cultural wisdom of eternities—is dismissed in the fracas of daily existing. Let's get it back.

Does just one deal, just one transaction, truly affect anything but our own small lives, our invisible existence, our routine of getting up, going to work, eating, sleeping, and doing it all again? When you die, doesn't the world just swallow up the place you occupied, filling it instantly with another expendable human being? Perhaps a human being you birthed?

And isn't it true that for a car saleswoman, for instance, not making this one deal with you won't really affect her life all that much? And if you don't get that car, or that job, or that client, you'll get another one, won't you?

What if it does matter? What if not making this one deal with you is all that separates her from losing her home? What if you don't get the car, the job, or this client? What if we acknowledge that it *does* matter? That *we* matter? A negotiation is a slice of your life. A convergence of forces ready to act in your favor, tipped toward success the moment you show up with the right intention. All the parties involved in the transaction are present now, lined up in time and space for the purpose of creating this one deal, this one overflow of abundance in the generous world in which we live.

Because all the people in the transaction are aligned, in harmony in time and space for this brief moment, doesn't that imply something significant to you?

Doesn't that imply that there couldn't be a more perfect time for this deal to come out perfectly, in its own perfect time, for the highest good of all concerned?

Because you've put the effort into being present at this precise moment at this exact location and you know what you want, it makes perfect sense that, if it is at all possible, the deal should work out ideally for everyone concerned.

Recognizing and capitalizing on those moments of negotiation is the purpose of this book. Not every deal will or should work out. There will be impasses, for certain. Some things just are "not meant to be" or are "impossible" by someone's standards. At times, you will be forced to deal with unenlightened cretins or unfortunate, blinded people who cannot be overwhelmed with your good intentions. In these cases, your dignity requires and your wisdom mandates that you walk away, wishing none ill.

But these cases are rare. They are unique. They are so unlikely in real life for an enlightened, empowered woman as to be almost nonexistent.

This book is designed to help you improve your competence in the practical skills of negotiation, but also to help you tap into the "Essential Feminine"—the power invested in you as a woman to help make the world a better place for everyone with whom you interact. Creating goodness in our big world comes back many times over in goodness for you. It makes your path smoother; it makes your journey easier.

While we've been negotiating all throughout our lives, I started negotiating professionally in 1989, when I first began working as a literary agent. Since then, I've negotiated more than 450 rights deals for books and other intellectual properties, in many countries worldwide. I've negotiated screenplay deals with Hollywood "shark" producers. I've argued with some pretty tough attorneys, and I've negotiated many book deals with kind, well-meaning editors who don't have a single negotiation skill. I've even negotiated my way through my own divorce, with amicable results.

In my years of negotiating and studying negotiating, I have learned a lot about the *people* side of negotiation, and have come to believe that the skills are wholly secondary to the people. There are many books that can teach you the basic practical skills. I'll even go over those skills in the pages that follow. But more importantly, the people skills are the greatest asset in a negotiation. The ability to intuitively understand where someone is coming from, the ability to use questions effectively, to find the "heart" of the deal, and to be in touch with what's really going on are critical skills. Luckily, they are the under-celebrated skills in which women tend to naturally excel. We just need to polish them until they shine.

Negotiation books are most often written by men, mostly attorneys and other men who see the territory of a negotiation as a "battleground" and talk about "win-win" as if that's a major shift of consciousness. I ask you, though, what woman wasn't 6 years old once and didn't realize that "win-win" was the best way to play Barbies? We all learned that sharing the doll with the prettiest hair was important if we wanted to keep our best friend.

We already know it's about win-win. How do we balance that desire with the desire for fairness and equity, especially when dealing with people who may not have our enlightened perspective?

As you explore these pages, learning from the wisdom of the women who have contributed their insights to this book, you will see that there is a way to handle every negotiation with honor, energy, dignity, and power. There's no reason to ever feel you got the short end of the stick again, or feel that horrible feeling signaling you took advantage of someone else. You won't be having those feelings anymore.

By the time you finish reading this book, you will be armed with the skills and clued into your own wisdom so that your negotiations are properly chosen, well executed, and clearly defined. You'll learn the overarching principles of negotiating—from a woman's perspective—and the day-to-day strategies to use to make sure your negotiations work to everyone's best advantage.

Negotiation Power

Every negotiation is a chance for you to prove to yourself, once again, that you are a wise, mature woman worthy of commanding from the abundance of the universe everything you want. By remaining calm, observing the situation, applying your intuition, and infusing the deal with a jolt of creativity, you have given yourself access to a power few can rival.

This book explores the elements of a good negotiation, both from a solid, practical skills level and from the higher level: the level of intention, dignity, power, and strength.

You are likely to surprise yourself as your attitude about negotiation now begins to change. You will find that things just seem to go smoother, more easily. People make way for you in the world. It isn't a constant battle, one-on-one combat as some male-oriented negotiation books would have you believe. The world isn't a dog-eat-dog place, unless your name is Rover or Spike. Women have the precious gift of being able to see under, through, around, above, inside, and beside every situation. When we apply this nearly magical skill to negotiations of all types, we tap into our power and are able to easily and resiliently create what we need from the world around us.

Let's begin the process of transformation. It begins in your heart and ripples through the world like a current the moment you begin to use it.

In Summary

Love is the ultimate negotiation tool.

CHAPTER 2

The
Bambi Effect

"This is my simple religion. There is no need for
temples; no need for complicated philosophy.
Our own brain, our own heart is our temple; the
philosophy is kindness."
—His Holiness the Dalai Lama

Mystics and New Thought people talk about karma—the accumulated result of one's actions in this and perhaps other (depending on to whom you're talking) lifetimes. Karma aside, it is logical to imagine that you can build up for yourself a storehouse of energy, positive or negative, by the actions you take today. Your dealings with other people—your *negotiations*—quickly amount to the quality of your life.

Businesses often have a "difficult customer" price and a "good customer" price, whether that's fair or not. Yelling at a customer service person on the phone somehow mysteriously gets you disconnected and then you have to wait on hold again to get through to anyone who will help you. Individuals respond to how you treat them, and individuals are what make a business or entity come to life. The simplest negotiation, asking the waitress to bring ketchup, can be done in a way that is kind and polite or a way that is rude and causes her to be resistant to your request. The essential power to transform the way you are treated stems from your power to treat others respectfully and with kindness.

You learned the biggest "trick" of negotiation as a little girl watching *Bambi*, of all things. Thumper's mother taught us a core truth of negotiation and human relationships. Ascribing this deep wisdom to Thumper's daddy, she asks Thumper what his father told him about dealing with other people. Thumper drawls, "If you can't say something nice, don't say anything at all."

Being a difficult customer, a difficult mother, a difficult spouse—frequently expressing the negative—of course brings you a world full of people who don't want to deal with you. Nothing works faster to increase the amount of stress in your life than to cause stress in other people's lives. The converse is also true. The results you manifest outside yourself come directly from the thoughts you hold inside and the actions you take outside. The choice, the power, the control is always in your hands.

Big Head, Small Mind

In 1988, when I was a young mother, I bought a charming little sweater and trouser set for my son at a ritzy boutique. He was growing fast, so I bought it a little large, in 3T. It should have been amply big. The charming, attentive Asian lady who ran the store repeated several times what a lovely outfit it was, and what a good choice I was making.

I paid more than I normally would have, because I was infatuated with how great it would look on my 18-month-old son, Jeremy. But when I got the outfit home and tried to put it over my son's head, I discovered the neck opening wasn't as big as a typical saucer, and it had no give.

I took it back to the boutique the next morning. I had Jeremy with me this time. The lady, in suddenly bad English, insisted she would not take it back. I showed her the intact tags, the receipt, the bag she had wrapped it in the afternoon before.

She shook her head. "Not my problem. You son have deformed head. Head too big. Not my problem."

We spent 10 minutes talking about the garment, Jeremy's really average-size head, and the poor service I was getting. She was adamant. I did not get a return, a refund, or an exchange. I was angry.

Shocked at her rudeness, I warned my girlfriends not to buy clothing for their children in the shop. The average unhappy customer tells 11 others. I am quite certain I told more people than that. Of course, the people I told didn't go there. Apparently no one else did, either. The store was closed within six months of the incident. I wonder how she felt when she failed in business. I'm sure it broke her heart. It would have broken mine.

If I met that woman on the street and she didn't remember me, I have a feeling she would have lamented that her beautiful shop with exquisite clothes failed because it was "in a bad area" or "customers don't buy nice clothes for their children in this town." Maybe she would have blamed the mall owners for not advertising, or maybe she eventually would have blamed herself. Maybe it occurred to her that there were many solutions that would have stopped me and all the other disgruntled customers from spreading the word that her store was a bad place in which to shop.

She had choices: She could have simply refunded my money; she could have offered me an exchange; she could have chosen not to insult my baby; she could have made a point of apologizing; she could have posted her no refunds, no returns policy; she could have invested the time I spent angry with her making the customer happy—even without loss or cost to herself. If she had given me a gift certificate, or an exchange, I would not have become a zealous opponent of her store. It was her choice to negotiate badly with me.

Did that one transaction matter? The simple garment cost me just under $50 retail. I will guess it probably cost her 10 percent of that wholesale. For the sake of a measly five bucks, she created yet another disgruntled customer. She couldn't see the big picture. She built up a wave of negative karma and eventually, it smothered her little shop. Because of a lot of angry $50 losses, she eventually lost her store. Maybe owning that store had been her dream. Maybe she was so hurt emotionally that she never opened another store again.

I lost that negotiation, and so did she. The cumulative effect: Jeremy wore clothes bought from other places, but in time, she lost her whole business. Who suffered more?

Creating Positive Dry Cleaning Karma

Lucky for us, we can create positive karma just as easily. Try walking cheerfully into the dry cleaners to pick up your order. Smile at the other customers and the people behind the counter. In your most cheery voice, ask for your clothes. *Funny how pleasantly that transaction went,* you think as you practically skip back to your car.

But let's assume you get there and you realize they've made a huge mistake and your favorite shirt is ruined. You bring back in the shirt. The same man is behind the counter. You explain the situation. Are you more or less likely to get his attention and perhaps even a result because you were cheerful and kind to him a few minutes earlier?

We all know how unlikely it will be for the dry cleaners to whip out $75 and hand it to you with their apologies. More likely they will try not to accept blame for the ruined shirt. Your negotiation begins the moment you ask someone else to do or give something. They have declined your initial request—that they hand you $75.

But is this the end? You can scream, shout, and flail. Will that get you the result? Thumper's mother comes to mind. "If you can't say something nice...." Instead of grabbing this guy by the neck and yelling at him, you say, "You know, I've been coming here for the past seven years. I've spent hundreds of dollars on dry cleaning at this location. This is the first time anything like this has happened. What can we do so you can keep my business?"

And then, as an artful and wise negotiator, you accept the natural pause. You are in control. You wait for his response.

He is a little surprised. The last person whose clothes they ruined is a big former football player and he used his physical size to intimidate this small dry cleaner owner into refunding the money. He's surprised you're being so calm. He says, "Okay lady, thank you for your business. But this shirt was like this when it came here. It's not our fault. It's poor quality."

You pause again, to show him that you listened to his statement. Gracefully, you say in a calm and even-tempered voice, "We need to do something about this. How do you propose we solve this problem?"

Asking questions puts control of the conversation in your hands. You are calm and balanced. You are not shrieking like the last woman whose shirt they ruined. He knows full well they did it, and so do you. You are restoring—even granting—him an opportunity to "save face," to do the right thing and appease you in the process.

Perhaps he'll refund the money for the shirt. Perhaps he'll refund the sum you just paid to have that shirt cleaned. Perhaps he's off center and he will yell at you that they don't need your business. Perhaps he'll give you a 20-percent discount on your next four orders. Perhaps he has no power or authority and will refer you to someone who does.

It may take some back and forth. If it's worth it to you, you may be willing to talk to the manager if he isn't the manager. You may be willing to never patronize them again. Or you may find that your courtesy and calm, polite-but-firm demeanor gets you exactly the result you prefer: the refund of the cost of the shirt.

Either way, you walk out the winner. A garment you have worn at least once before today is no longer wearable, but you have either identified an establishment at which you will no longer do business (or risk your other clothes), or you have reached a fair agreement. You may have had a different outcome if you had been a customer noted for her bad attitude in the months preceding the incident. Who knows?

"If you scatter thorns, don't go barefoot."
—Italian proverb

It's a *Very* Small World After All

People tend to have a lot of fear about negotiations. Assume you're visiting a foreign country. You look like any other American tourist. You see the most beautiful leather purse. It would cost a fortune at home for something of this quality. You adore it. You negotiate with the seller. You end up getting a real deal on it. You're nearly gloating as you carry it home. You paid a better than fair price, and in fact you are pretty certain you got a steal.

When you get back home, you show it to a friend who just happens to be a native of the country you visited. She asks you what you paid. When you tell her, she laughs and says, "You paid the 'tourist price'!" She proves to you that your new bag isn't all real leather, it's part plastic, despite the "verra pelle" label. How do you feel about your steal now? Not so good.

Try this: Your house is up for sale. Your real estate agent advises you to list it for top dollar. To your great surprise, it sells within a week for your full asking price. You're delighted and joyful at your good fortune. But two months later, you find out the buyer is a corporation who knew in advance that due to some zoning changes, your property is now worth five times more than even the high price they paid for it.

Now imagine you own a little company. While you do a fair business, there's one client who annoys you to no end. She's always got to have a little more attention than everyone else. She doesn't know you charge her an extra 20 percent for the annoyance factor over what you charge everyone else. What harm can it do?

Two months later, she happens to be talking to her friend over lunch, who tells her that she was overcharged for your services. The two of them figure out what you were doing. Bad news. Her lunch partner writes a business column for the local newspaper.

Most experts claim there are two kinds of negotiations in the world: the kind in which one party wins while the other party loses, and the kind in which both parties win. Women know there's a third: the negotiation in which *everyone* loses.

While we don't want to victimize others, we also do not wish to become victims. We all fear getting charged too much by the mechanic. We all know there have been times when we came out ahead and someone else lost in a negotiation with us. If you stop for a moment and think about it, it's quite obvious that neither being taken advantage of nor taking advantage of someone else feels right. Neither offers long-term benefits for either party involved.

Women have innumerable advantages in negotiations. We can use a multitude of natural inbred skills that few men can access. But we have another, larger advantage, too. We have the power to use real, honest win-win negotiations to create a better world for ourselves and our children, beginning right here, right now.

The Bible says, "The laborer is worthy of her hire." (Luke 10:7, New American Standard Version, revised.)

The Koran says, "They were entitled to it and worthy of it." (The Victory 48:26)

The Torah says, "In all labor there is profit; but the talk of the lips tends only to penury." (Proverb 14)

By being fair to yourself and to others in all your negotiations, you will improve your little corner of the world. Like a pebble dropped in a still pond, the ripple effect will be huge when your ripple hits the ripples of the women all around you who are negotiating from strength, integrity, and calm power.

This book is about showing you how you can tap into that power. You have a responsibility to yourself, your children, and your planet to begin at once to get what you want in the right way, while giving people what they want fairly in return. It's time to release your inner strength to heal relationships, to protect yourself and your family, and to do a fair day's work for a fair day's wage. Your ability to negotiate will transform every aspect of your life.

You negotiate every day with the people around you. From the dry cleaner that accidentally tore the buttons off your best coat to the teenager holed up and refusing to clean his bedroom, from the customer standing before you to the waitress who served you dinner, we are constantly negotiating at some level with every person with whom we interact. Learning to do that in a win-win way guarantees your success in every negotiation, both in the moment and in the long run. And after all, it's the long run that really matters.

In Summary

What you put out comes back. You get to choose.

CHAPTER 3

Pick
Your Peaches

"An apple is an excellent thing...until you have
tried a peach."
—George du Maurier,
artist, novelist (1834-1896)

Why is it so difficult to pick the perfect peach from the grocery
store? They all look so pretty, displayed on the produce rack. Blushing
in a hundred sunset hues of orange, yellow, and pink, they each look
perfect, delectable, and juicy.

Like every woman does, you pick the best-looking one up and
give it a squeeze. It's not ripe. The next one you choose you know is
going to be mealy. How long have these been here, anyway? That one
is bruised—probably rolled across the floor yesterday. This one is gushy.
You gently place a few in your thin plastic bag, hoping for the best. Or
you pass on the whole lot, having been burned by buying bad peaches
here before. And who returns peaches? I've thrown half a dozen in the
trash, one by one. Who hasn't?

Picking good fruit is very similar to good negotiation. You have to
make choices based on what you want, what's really important to you.
The shorthand, although more male expression, is "pick your battles"—
which is to say, decide what's worth expending your energy on.

If returning $4 worth of peaches is worth it to you, you'll take them back, whether it's to prove a point to the manager or because you need the $4. I once saw a very successful businessman walk on a $250 matter that I personally would have brought to someone's attention and tried to negotiate, but to him the money was the same as the $4 refund for the bad peaches would be to another person. It's a matter of what you can tolerate, what you can handle, what's worth it to you. You get to decide.

> "We are here on earth to do good to others.
> What the others are here for, I don't know."
> —W.H. Auden, American poet, 1907-1973

Bad Days, Bad Eggs, and Jazz Shoes

Some days, it seems unlikely that there are not more wars, divorces, and killing sprees.

Today, in the simple act of trying to pick the perfect new publicist to work for my company, I spoke to half a dozen people who interviewed in my office. They were entering a negotiation with me when they walked in—a negotiation for a job. One would assume that they would have been prepared, in best form, ready to be chosen. They would be the best-looking peaches on the shelf.

If they could have seen themselves, surely they would have been as shocked and disgusted as I was by 5 p.m.

First, there came the fat, sloppy woman who wore clothes I wouldn't wear shopping at Home Depot. She spent two-thirds of the interview apologizing for forgetting what she saw on our Website the day before. I didn't ask. She brought it up.

There was the ditzy ex-New Yorker who talked without taking a breath for fully 15 minutes about how much she loved and missed her old job. Then she asked me what the job I was offering paid and when she would be entitled to full-time employee benefits. I reminded her that this was a part-time permanent position, and that the information was all given on the ad listing. She suddenly got up, fussed with her hair, and left. She didn't apologize for taking my time, she just simply kept repeating on her way out that if I ever wanted to make the position full time with benefits, she would be interested. I am not.

I was silently amused by the applicant who told me that I didn't know how to run my business, and instead her idea of handing things out for free at a business fair was the best way to promote my company. It isn't.

My late grandfather would have said they were all "bad eggs." These were just three out of six interviews, and that's bad enough. No more needs to be said about the process of hiring someone. I wish every applicant could imagine what the person conducting the interview sees in a day. Is it a matter of picking the least offensive candidate or the most desirable candidate? Like any negotiation, it depends on what's more important to me, time vs. money vs. energy. Because I had the time, I kept looking until I was able to negotiate a hiring contract with the ideal person. Had it been a less important position in my company, or had I less time, I would have just chosen someone out of those I was offered that awful day.

No matter which side of the negotiation you are on, your choices always have to be realistic. You may not always find the best deal, but the best deal considering all the factors nonetheless. Is it worth the time to return the bad peaches to the store? Is it worth the money? Will you feel righteous in proving to them their produce is poor? What a "good" deal looks like to one person is very different from what one might look like to another.

As if to remind me of the dark side of business life, I drive home the night of the horrible interviews and pick my child up at school. It's time for her Monday night dance class. We go inside the dancing school. The consistently vacuous woman who badly administers the dance studio is behind the desk. We have five years of misunderstanding one another behind us. I cannot fathom why the studio owner, a bright, dear woman who spends most of her time teaching the little ballerinas, tolerates her assistant's whining, incompetence, and bad customer service practices. I am grateful I don't have an employee like her. She's always mired in some personal problem, always can't find the pen or the paper or the change or something.

I ask her if we can look at the jazz dance shoes, which are locked in a display case at the other end of the lobby. She says yes, stands up, and walks 20 feet to the case. She points through the glass. "Those are the jazz shoes," she says.

I tell her I know and that I wish to see a pair in size 8. She says flatly that she can't open the case. I ask why not. She says the key is in her desk. She walks back across the floor, gets the key, scowling at me on her round trip. She gives The Look (indicating my troublesome nature) to some waiting mothers clustered around her desk asking questions such as, "What time does the 6 p.m. jazz class start?"

Now I am nearly out of patience. Nothing is ever simple with this woman. She opens the case. She pulls out pink canvas ballet shoes and lifts them for my inspection. I say, "We need jazz shoes, please."

She says, "Well, these are ballet shoes." I know that. The jazz shoes are 6 inches from her hand.

I say as calmly as I can, "We need the black ones, the jazz shoes."

She is annoyed. She says, "I can't show them to you until you tell me what size she needs."

I tell her size 8. Again.

She says, "That's all you had to do, just tell me the size, you know."

She pulls out piles of ballet shoes, rummages through the stack of black jazz shoes, and finally comes across a pair that look nothing like the ones I requested except that they are also black. She tells me, "Try these. They are size 7 1/2 but maybe you can get her foot in them."

My daughter takes them and cannot squeeze her foot into them. I ask her whether they can order them.

She says, "Yes, but our orders don't come in until Tuesday."

I say fine, and that we'd like to order them.

She says, "We can't get those kind in. We don't order those."

I thank her, for what I do not know, and ask her if she knows where they sell them. She seems to randomly name a city at least 20 miles away, vaguely telling me, "See if there's a dance store there."

I want to scream in frustration. I want to walk the 10 feet to her boss, a nice but overworked woman, and tell her that for the 300th time her employee has proven to be utterly incompetent. Of course, I say nothing. The woman who runs the studio probably knows. Maybe she allows this woman to work for her because she can't find anyone else, or doesn't have time. She's made a negotiation of it. She's probably negotiated with herself and her life, determined that it's too much trouble to fire, advertise, select, and train another employee, so she tolerates the one she has. However inept she may be.

Two weeks later, the exact shoes we asked for in my daughter's size are in the case. I hand my 11-year-old some cash and let her deal with the transaction. She gets the shoes.

Honestly, I loathe the fact that my daughter takes lessons here, but the reason she does is that it is the only dance studio in our small town. I've negotiated with my life and realized that the drive to school to pick up my child, then out of our town to the next closest dance studio, and then home again means about an extra hour and a half in the car each week.

Despite my frustrations and her boss's, the attendant at the dance studio keeps her job. I pause to think about it, and realize she has given me fodder for this very book.

How often in life do we have to deal with a mentally deficient, incomprehensible, totally bored, or utterly incompetent employee who is working for someone with whom we want to or must do business? How many times in life are we accosted by some underling who placidly tells us we cannot have what we want, that they cannot do as we wish because of "store policy" or some other string of frustrating, stupid reasons why the simplest acts cannot be done? "We can't refund your money on this defective product because we only refund on Tuesdays between 3 and 4 a.m."

The answer is far, far more often than we like. If we were the Waltons, we would only have to deal with Ike at the general store. We would have to like him, or at least be civil, because he would be all there is. But in a culture where we have so many options of where, when, and how we expect service, we also interact with a far greater number of service providers. We negotiate with them for service. From asking for no onions on your hamburger to asking if they can finish the repainting of your home's exterior before Christmas, all our life has become a series of negotiations. And how you deal with these negotiations determines the quality of your life.

"A person who can't lead and won't follow
makes a dandy roadblock."
—Richard Zera

I walk out of the dance studio and into a coffee shop, part of a well-known chain. This is where I often sit and write during dance classes. Today a new employee is at the counter. The store must have daily staff turnover. In seven years, only once have I seen the same employee twice in this shop. I ask her for mint tea that is not too hot, please, with a little ice in it, requesting five cubes.

She smiles and nods. A hundred employees before her have smiled and nodded when I asked for mint tea cooled with ice cubes. I used to ask for half cold, half hot water, until a college boy told me that "tea is all water with just one tea bag." No kidding. I have asked before quite specifically for five ice cubes to be put into the cup. I have been told every reason why I cannot have that, or worse, told it was done and it wasn't. I know that tonight, I have about a one-in-100 chance of getting tea that won't scorch my mouth.

I see her add a bit of ice to it. Hope is revived. I can't tell how much ice from where I stand. I see her smile as she puts the lid on. Cautiously, I lift it to my lips, ready to be scalded yet again. It's perfect! She has created the perfect temperature. She listened to what I requested and complied! I am joyful, grateful, and happy.

Here's the part that applies directly to negotiations. In the case of the incompetent dancing school secretary, I did nothing but be annoyed for a few minutes. In the case of the rare, semiprecious coffee barista, I did nothing, either. I didn't put more than 20 percent of the price of the coffee—a quarter—in the tip jar. I probably won't write the corporate headquarters to compliment them on this employee, because, whether I do or not, she's probably majoring in nuclear physics or theology at the local university and doesn't care whether she keeps the job at the coffee chain.

I still take my daughter to dance class, although I typically drop her off in front, partly so I don't have to deal with the beastly woman at the front desk. They still get my business. They still get my money. I still go to the coffee shop, despite endless scaldings.

Common wisdom says customers vote with their dollars. It's often true when they think they have a choice. Henry Ford reputedly said that new car buyers could have any color car they wanted as long as it was black. You can't win 'em all. How much does this encounter really matter in the overall happiness level of your life?

In matters of negotiation, I simply do not have the energy to train other people's employees after spending the day training my own. I have become accustomed to incompetence and am surprised by real service. Most Americans would agree, I'm sure.

There is no real benefit to trying to get every irritating situation to become a smoother one. This entire episode from bad interviewees to perfect tea happened during the course of less than 10 hours of my life. While I would love to be treated well in every transaction of my life, I recognize the improbability of this. It's like child rearing—you have to pick your battles.

The December 2003 issue of *Self* magazine promises that we can all get treated like a celebrity—red carpet treatment—if we only remember to say "please" and "thank you" and be gracious. Try that next time you call tech support for your software. There's a whole lot more to negotiation and getting your way than just being gracious. There are plenty of "little people" to step over, deal with, maneuver around, and negotiate through before you get anything accomplished.

Proverbially, you have to butter up the secretary to get to the boss.

You have to be nice to the person who takes your order at Taco Bell because heaven only knows what they could do to your food if you're rude. (I know, one of my relatives worked in fast food.)

If the benefit is worth the hassle of negotiation, pull out all the stops. Negotiate away! Use your skills to be the empowered, calm, dominant, well-prepared woman you are. Charm, flirt, kill them with kindness. There's no harm in getting the job done. Just pick your battles. If there is no benefit to you when dealing with an incompetent person, just let it go. A big part of negotiation is applying your skills to things that really matter, not to petty things that don't. There's only so much of you to go around.

The theory of a negotiation book is that once read, it will solve all your problems. The dry cleaners will never ruin your clothes again, your mate will suddenly be putty (or steel) in your hands, and your life will be strewn with roses.

I hate reading books that tell me if I expend enormous, consistent effort, my life will suddenly be perfect. Forget it. It won't. You can have all the skills and noble ideals you like. You'll still deal with minimum wage wastrels and people who couldn't care less if you never do business there again.

Negotiation is about creating and pursuing your objectives when those objectives matter to you enough to take the energy it takes to create them.

Your teenager is using drugs *and* doesn't make her bed. Which battle will you pitch?

Your 4-year-old doesn't want to eat broccoli *and* bites the other kids at preschool. Which battle will you pitch?

Your mate never, ever puts the toothpaste away *and* is having sex with the next door neighbor. Which battle will you pitch?

Your boss asks you to work overtime every single evening *and* has recently cut out all your health benefits. Which battle will you pitch?

In every case, you have to make a choice. Maybe it seems obvious to you, but you can't win 'em all. Kindness greases the wheels that make the world turn, but in this hurried, frantic, stressed-out society, you can't negotiate everyone into doing, seeing, and completing things your way.

In Summary

Pick what's important enough to negotiate and let the rest go. Many things fall in the "life's too short" category. Focus on the things that matter.

CHAPTER 4

There's Enough for Everybody

"If you know that everything coming your way can be used for your good, you don't need to be afraid of what might look difficult. You can relax into the fact that there will always be challenges and difficulties because life is a progressive process of growth and understanding. Accepting this will allow you use your energy to have more of what you want in your life instead of using it up praying for the day when difficult things will stop happening. That day will not come."
—Marilyn Graman and Maureen Walsh,
The Female Power Within

It Matters

The seminar room was precisely half full of shouting, angry people. Some stood on their padded metal chairs and yelled. A few sat quietly in their chairs, some fuming, and some rocking themselves consumed by inner rage. A girl in her early 20s was crying loudly. A middle aged woman stood up, walked over to the mousy young man who was speaking, and yanked the blue dry erase marker out of his hand.

"You're wrong!" she shouted. Several people cheered her on from the seats. The guy with the tattoos shook his fist at her.

She said, "It's not like this at all. You're an idiot!" She smeared away everything he had written on the dry erase board with the sleeve of her red shirt. She began a diagram with circles and arrows and lines. A man booed her and told her to sit down. She gave him the finger. Two people rushed the stage and started shouting with her.

No, this wasn't Jerry Springer. It wasn't even acrimonious, until now. No one watching would believe that half an hour earlier, 98 calm, professional people had been sitting quietly in a seminar room in a nondescript Los Angeles suburb waiting to hear instructions for the "red/black" game. The rules were simple. The instructor had said, "I'm going to split you into two even groups. Your goal is to win the game. You have one hour." He explained how to get points, and that we would be required to vote unanimously on 10 squares on a board. We had to vote to color the square red or black each time, one by one. If we voted red and the other team voted black, they would win. But if they voted red, too, we'd both lose. If they voted red and we voted black, we'd get the points. He took no questions, despite our confusion. He left the room with 49 people, precisely half our number. We were kept in separate rooms with no contact between the groups.

Sixty minutes and much shouting, cursing, and even crying later, the other half of the group came back in. They were angry, too, it seemed. They had fought with one another also. They sat down. The instructor stood up shaking his head, scolding us for our selfishness.

"You just spent an hour trying to guess what they were voting—a bunch of total strangers—so that you could beat them." He sounded disappointed in our performance. "If you had voted black at each option on the board, you would have won the game—and so would the other team." He took a long sigh and shook his head at us. "How you play this game is how you play your life. You think it doesn't matter to vote "black" in life—to vote win-win? Think about it. It matters. It always matters." He sent us home in silence to think about it. By being greedy and trying so hard to "win," both teams had lost.

We hung our heads in silence, and plodded out of the room to rethink our approach. We were each trying so hard not just to beat the team in the other room, but to enforce our idea of how the game should be played. We lost all dignity, all civility, all sense of right, logic, and fairness. We had cut ourselves adrift from common sense, and fomented anger in a room full of people we barely knew.

Sure, it's human nature to want to win. It's human nature to try to get just a tiny bit more than the other party has. And what if you give in but the other side cheats? What if they don't keep their end of the bargain? You'll feel like a fool.

Who hasn't felt buyer's remorse? Find one person who hasn't bought something and regretted it because it was junk and we could never get our money back. I know 20 people who don't trust human nature enough to do business on eBay because, "What if the other person takes my money and never sends the item?" As a seller on eBay, I had someone get the merchandise, claim they didn't, and then insist on a refund. I sent her the money. Heck, it's her karma not mine, and my good reputation on eBay, not hers.

Our goal, as skillful negotiators, is to rise above the caveman mentality of fear-based negotiations. The idea of "losing out" is such a powerful tactic, companies often sell intentionally limited quantities of an item to trigger our fear of losing out, of not getting our fair share, of someone getting more than us.

Remember when you were a kid and you fought with your siblings about who got the bigger dessert? Smart moms let one kid do the cutting, and the other chooses first. Desserts have been perfectly equal down to the last sugar molecule ever since!

More for Kenmore

Jan Austin, one of the nation's leading and most effective female business coaches (*www.brandyourself.com*), told me the following story about creating a bigger pie, about "voting black," about seeing abundance, about making a deal work for everyone without anyone losing anything:

"My husband and I sold a house we had. We were using a brand new Realtor. I think this was his first sale.

"The woman who wanted to buy our house is a single mom. She'd qualified to buy under a federal program. We'd asked a no-nonsense price. She seemed to agree. But suddenly, the negotiations stalled.

"I asked the Realtor what was wrong. He didn't have an answer. He wasn't even clued in to what was going on. I asked him again, 'What does she really need?' He went off and asked her Realtor. It turned out, she wanted cash for appliances.

"I told the Realtor he should have anticipated this. I told him, 'You left it to me to find out what she really needs. What she was really worried about was the appliances, and how she would afford them.'" *Jan was thinking about what the new owner needed, not just about herself.*

"We were able to find a way for her to get money at the close of escrow for the appliances she needed. I always listen for what other people need. The biggest mistake I see is people being rigid in negotiations. You have to apply some creativity.

"Meeting other people halfway doesn't mean you have to compromise what you really want. Giving them what they need may not cost you anything, as in the case of the house we sold to the single mom.

"If we only guess what the other party wants, we won't come in reasonably. We're likely to increase the emotional quotient. This will cause emotional thinking and take us out of rational thinking. That will undermine the entire negotiation."

🐾 🐾 🐾

Jan's story reminds us that creating a deal that makes both sides happy is not only the goal of negotiation, it is also usually possible and in everyone's best interests.

We're grown-ups now. **The first principle of successful negotiation is to humbly recognize that we live in a world overflowing with abundance.**

We can choose to believe in the beneficence of the universe around us and give generously. We can give fairly. We can solve our negotiation challenges by considering what the other person really wants, what they really need. By giving a little more, by being flexible, we can create many more "done deals" with fewer bad feelings and move through our lives reaping the many benefits of our attitude of abundance consciousness.

Sticking on your stubborn sense of entitlement makes you as surly as the people screaming in the seminar room. Remember to sway, to see things from the other person's perspective.

Erich Schiffmann, 1992 Yoga Teacher of the Year and powerful master teacher on the award-winning yoga video, *Yoga Mind & Body* with Ali McGraw speaks during "tree pose." He admonishes us to stay rooted, grounded, but to remember that "it's all right to sway. Trees sway." It is the ability to sway that keeps the trees from breaking in heavy winds.

When you acknowledge the abundance of your life, of the universe in which we all live, the abundance of our country, the beauty of nature, the joy of a hot bubble bath, the sound of a child's merry laugh, the gentle, exquisite form of a flower, you see abundance surrounding you at all times, in every way. Touching this precious abundance, you are a part of it. Sharing this abundance in negotiation, in a way that is fair and wholesome for all concerned, is what makes you a supremely good negotiator.

In Summary

The other person in the negotiation matters as much as you do. To win, you need to consider the best interests of all parties involved. There's plenty for everybody. This attitude reflects your awareness of the abundance of all around you.

CHAPTER 5

Principles
of Negotiation

"A powerful woman is aware of her strengths and
talents, and lives with them as a matter of fact.
A powerful woman uses all her experiences for
her well-being."
— Marilyn Graman and Maureen Walsh,
The Female Power Within

Extreme Behavior

There seem to be two extremes of thought on negotiation. One is, "Let's take 'em for everything they've got and leave the desiccated corpse on the floor as we leave." The other is more along the lines of, "Oh, well, he was such a nice man, and I felt sorry for him because his kid has cerebral palsy and his wife left him. I just couldn't bring myself to drive a hard bargain." It's mostly us women who waiver between the two approaches: leaving too much on the table and demanding things we just can't have.

The most important skill you can learn is to always negotiate from a position of inner strength, personal power, wisdom, and dignity.

In the 1979 movie *Kramer vs. Kramer*, a mother abandons her child. After a year and a half, she returns to claim custody, having "straightened out" her mind and life. The attorneys for each party drag the other parent through the mud, yanking out tactics and vicious negotiation strategies that wound the other. Bleeding emotionally, the court leaves her victorious and in primary custody of their child, but she is so pained by her own negotiation tactics, her own decisions, that she, in the end, decides to leave their son in the care of his dad. Although she got what she wanted, the victory was hollow.

Most of the negotiation books I can find are written by men who eviscerate other people for a living (attorneys, wheeler-dealers, ruthless and cunning businessmen). Somehow, this gives them ultimate credibility to teach others how to do the same.

As an adult, I negotiate for a living. I negotiate contracts every day for authors and speakers, helping them put their message in front of the right people. The industries I work in—publishing, media, speaking, and meetings—are interesting because I negotiate with at least as many women as men. This gives me a chance to see the styles and patterns of individuals and genders. Formerly, I sold screenplays in Hollywood, where the negotiations are often cutthroat, and something invisible is always lurking behind the deal.

I've learned that if I want to do business again with someone or their establishment, I've got to make fair deals for everyone concerned. I have worked in *relationship-based* industries. That means I sell different things to the same people over and over again, but I am also always bringing in new contacts and clients, negotiating with them as well. No matter whether it was a "one shot" negotiation or a negotiation with a colleague with whom I've worked for decades, I have seen, over and over again, that there is nothing sweeter than a fair deal fairly won.

You can't afford to create a situation where the "loser" in the negotiation watches you as you triumphantly stride away, saying to him- or herself, "What a powerful negotiator she is! She cut my head off. You've got admire a woman like that!" Success is about having the other party—your boss, your client, your customer, your kid, your spouse—want to "transact business" with you again. You want to keep the relationship intact and still be able to know in your heart and mind that you not only got a fair deal, but so did the other party.

The second principle in negotiation is to create a situation in which both parties feel their needs are being served, where both sides feel that, while they may not have gotten the *best* deal, they certainly got a fair one.

Your Natural Skills

As babies, we negotiated for survival at the most primal level. "You feed me, care for me, and cuddle me and in return I'll coo and smile at you." It was instinctive, but good negotiations always come from finely honed instincts. Skills are less important than learning "the real deal" and playing by its real rules.

As girls, many of us learned negotiation when we were still in pigtails. Whether it was batting your eyelashes at a doting daddy or being able to charm your mother into buying you just one more new outfit, many girls learn emotional negotiation at a very early age. Getting that new Barbie was easier if you asked the right adult, and you always knew which one to ask, didn't you?

Somehow, you figured out how to signal to a boy at school that you liked him. You watched, you learned, you repeated behaviors with your body, your eyes, your shy smile, until you found a technique that really worked for you.

As an adult, you were able to woo your employer into giving you the job instead of someone else. Don't kid yourself. Set aside the hiring and management books that proclaim people hire people for skills only. If you were rude and abrasive in the interview but had MIT or Harvard on your resume, you'd still be walking the pavement. You negotiated your way into the job, using a combination of winning personality skills and whatever qualifications got you the interview.

You already have the core skills you need to become a great negotiator. You may be lacking a little confidence, a larger perspective, or even some valuable skills. When you close this book, you'll be a pro.

Flexible Negotiations

I remember the first time I felt the rush of competition. It was 1976, and newspaper delivery girls were still a rare phenomenon. I think there were three newspaper girls and more than 50 boys in my part of Cook County, Ill. My parents gave me permission to get up at 5:30 a.m. in the icy Chicago winter and roll papers. I'd then drag them down the driveway and load them into my shiny metallic green bicycle with the white banana seat, and throw one to each house on my route. It was hard work, but I felt the thrill of independence. I think I was paid 25 cents per week per house.

The paper decided to run a contest. Whichever kid got the most new subscribers could win prizes and money. I had to win. I knew instantly as I listened to the contest details that I would win, that I would show all these boys I was as good as they were, that I would earn money and presents for my two brothers. I began selling subscriptions in my route area right away.

Back then, little girls could still safely knock on doors. I learned negotiation and sales on the snow-covered doorsteps of my neighborhood. First, I had to look for a car to be in the driveway, fresh tire tracks in the snow, or a light on inside the house. That's how you knew someone was home. When I knocked, I stood back from the top step—so that the first moments wouldn't be spent with some grown-up apologizing for knocking me backward when he or she opened the door.

I smiled and spoke clearly. I nodded my head for absolutely no reason. I explained briefly and succinctly what I wanted. I looked them in the eye, smiled, and asked for the sale. This was picked up through trial and error. I didn't control subscription costs, but I could control my pitch. It seemed I had no negotiation room. It seemed like straight sales, but it wasn't. Each customer wanted something different.

Mr. Brown wanted his paper in plastic every day, rain or shine. "Can you do that, Wendy?"

"Sure, Mr. Brown."

The old couple two blocks down wanted me to *place* it on the stoop, not throw it from my bike. "Can you do that, Wendy?"

"Certainly, Mrs. Hammerschlad." It meant a dismount, which cost time, but it was worth it to me.

Mrs. Thomas insisted I throw it only onto the walkway, never on the lawn. "Will you promise me that, Wendy?"

"Of course, Mrs. Thomas."

Then there were the folks who said no. "I'm getting the other paper" or "I don't read the paper. Don't care what's going on." In those cases, it was a matter of deciding if the no was a maybe or if the no was a no.

This lead me to observe, directly, **the third principle of negotiation: Successful negotiation usually requires a big dose of creativity to make it work.**

You probably do this already in your personal life. Your significant other asks you if you want to go see a new action movie. You say no, and suggest a syrupy romance. He almost chokes. You decide on a fun romantic comedy you both enjoy. It was a tiny negotiation, with little at stake, but you both won. Fair deal.

Your 10-year-old is insistent that his bedtime is too early. You think it's about seven hours too late. He demands he be allowed to stay up until 10. You negotiate and agree on 9 p.m., *if* he takes a shower, washes his hair and brushes his teeth. Deal.

Negotiation is a part of your life you already know how to do. It's give a little, take a little. We do it all the time in our personal relationships. It's just a matter of applying those skills to business.

In Summary

"Creativity" means being flexible. Think of alternate ways you and the other party can get what you each want.

CHAPTER 6

Alpha Male
Negotiation Tactics

"All serious revolutionaries realize that power must be effectively, and sometimes ruthlessly, exercised if the revolution is to succeed…"
—Michael Ledeen,
Machiavelli on Modern Leadership

Tonight, I received a call from a male friend. He's a sweet, somewhat passive, average looking doctor on the East Coast. He told me his life has been revolutionized because he went to a seminar, learned the concept of the "alpha male," and now he is becoming one.

I listened, amused. He tells me that the seminar leader told the all-male audience that "women like men to be men." In his retelling, he explains there are "five things a woman wants in a man." Off the top of my head, I think I can list 500, but I allow him to continue uninterrupted.

The five things he tells me women want from a man are:

1. Dominance.
2. Decisiveness.
3. Sense of humor.
4. Compassion/empathy.
5. Kindness.

In his explanation of dominance, he tells me that it means that the man makes the decisions for the couple, and then sticks to his choices.

While all women know that this list is *partly* right, we obviously also see it is inherently *partly* wrong. The purpose of this book isn't to dissect a woman's needs in a relationship with a man. Unless of course she's sitting across the negotiation table from him or is trying to achieve what she wants during a late-night phone call. But I see an immediate parallel between the "alpha male" described above and the competent, confident negotiator.

I note that when I am negotiating with a true "alpha male" (as per my friend's definition) who wants his first book published, I will often tell him that his book is worse than it really is, or point out its many flaws more brusquely than I would if I were speaking to a "softer" male or another woman. This is because I am establishing primacy in my territory—publishing. It's like a gorilla beating his chest, or a lowly meerkat stretching itself to its tallest height to prove its right to lead the pack. By getting an alpha male's attention as a reputable authority, I move out of the category of "female" and into the category of someone this male respects.

My guy friend asks me if women do the "alpha female" thing with one another. I tell him that we do, but that I notice that once the "pecking order" is established, we don't really think much about it. We just get on with the task, the relationship, and our lives. I am reminded of elk, jaguars, chimps, or other beasts. The females have their own social order, and they really remain rather orderly within it. Each female is given her place, and pretty much accepts it. The males on the other hand constantly push. They lock horns. They challenge the leader, over and over, to see if he has aged and is ready to step down from his position.

As females, we already know in our hearts whether we are "alpha females" or more submissive females. The "alpha females" are often spurned with titles like "ball-buster" or "bitch" or "ice queen" or worse. This is because their ability to maintain their hierarchy is more similar to a male's than the traditional secondary psychosocial role assigned to females in a group situation.

The more submissive types of females are more able to be used for the benefit of the alphas. The other women are "cruel" to her, they "bully" her, the men treat her with no respect, they give her no attention, or the wrong kind of attention. These are all positions of weakness.

Whether you are an "alpha female" or a "submissive female," the trick to success is rapidly finding a balance between the two. This does not need to carry over into your personal relationships, unless that is part of your goal. But when it comes to negotiations with others, those outside your "pack" or "tribe," you most certainly want to adopt the practices of the alpha female while maintaining the innate charisma of your feminine power.

Perhaps you consider this easier said than done. But think back on the alpha male my doctor friend is becoming. The first characteristic is dominance. There's a big difference between "dominance" and "domineering." Domineering means to be a tyrant and be overbearing, but "dominance" simply means to govern or control a situation or person. You want to choose to be dominant.

The easiest way to behave in a way others see as dominant, even if it doesn't come naturally for you, is to recognize there are some very basic core components to dominance.

The first is your physicality. Have you ever noticed the way a police officer stands when he asks for your registration and you glumly pull it out of the glove box? They are trained to stand in a somewhat aggressive, certainly dominant position. Their body language exudes, "Don't mess with me!" The gun on their holster helps complete the ensemble, for certain, but even a chubby or a short and extremely thin officer can get away with terrifying most people. The uniform, the weapon, the power invested by the governing agency, these all contribute and are important. But reduce it simply to the officer's stance for a moment.

Imagine the officer is a female.

Imagine the officer is a female precisely your mother's age when you were 10 years old.

Imagine the officer looks just like your mom did when you were 10 years old and broke her most valuable vase.

Now, is it the badge and the gun that scare you, or is it the stance and the authority?

It's the stance and the authority. You can replicate this in your own situation, in any negotiation. This may seem hard to believe, but for as long as I've been in sales (more than 28 years and counting), I've been told to smile into the phone because people can pick up my body language without seeing me. In 28 years, I've come to *know*, beyond any shadow of a doubt, this is true. Body language communicates power.

So, imagine you are in a negotiation by phone. Stand up. Imitate the way your mother or Officer Friendly would stand. Breathe the way the officer or dear old mom would breathe if he or she were intent, 100-percent intent, on getting his or her way.

The transformation is remarkable, isn't it? Even the meekest woman can change the way others deal with her if she simply takes the physical posture of authority and control. It's nothing short of dominance! Try that the next time you discover the plumber breaks something while working, and see if you don't only get a reduction, but the value of the item paid to you at once!

Dominance has other components, too. Let's go back to you, your mom, and the broken vase. Was your mom's tone of voice when she was angry the same one she used when she read you a bedtime story? Of course not. My 11-year-old daughter Sophia told me just today that she likes the sound of my voice, just not "that voice." "That voice" means the one I use when I say her whole name in a tone that means she's in trouble—serious trouble.

Vocal inflection and the power behind our words make a big difference in establishing dominance. Whispering, sweet, soft voices are perfect for the bedroom and for talking to your babies. If that's your normal voice on the phone, you're in trouble. If that's the voice you use at the car dealership when insisting they lower your payment on the new car by $75 a month, you are probably in trouble again.

The easiest way to find your most powerful voice is through the practice of meditation. Coincidentally, when you sound your strongest is when you are speaking from your truest voice. To find this voice, take four very deep breaths. In through your nose, out fully and completely through your parted lips.

Now repeat the four breaths, this time inhaling for a count of seven, holding for a count of seven, and exhaling for a count of 14.

Immediately after "waking up" your lungs in this manner, inhale deeply again. Now allow the sound "Aaahhh" or "Om" to escape your mouth. Repeat. Drop your voice another octave. Repeat. Allow your sound to just be what it is, until it tickles the inside of your nose and makes your lungs shiver. This is your real voice, the voice of authority and strength. It's "I am woman, hear me roar."

This is the voice to use when you are in a negotiation: relaxed, powerful, centered, in control. When you get upset, your voice raises. The more upset you get, typically the higher your voice gets. By repeating this breathing exercise moments before you walk into a negotiation, you will center your voice deep within. The resonance of your true voice will give you the dominance and control you need to assert your position clearly. Physical stance, vocal quality, and choosing powerful words give power in negotiations.

Decisiveness is a core component of being seen by the other parties as dominant. Knowing what your outcome will be, what you want from the negotiation, is an invaluable advantage. You must know what success looks like for you to achieve it in any aspect of life. The next chapter dissects the principles of decisiveness and shows you how to create a decision for yourself and the situation prior to the actual negotiation.

In Summary

Different situations call for you to use different tools, even different parts of your personality, to succeed. As a competent negotiator, you will quickly assess and adjust your approach to suit the situation and to gain your outcome.

CHAPTER 7

Know
What You Want

"Women want men, careers, money, children, friends, luxury, comfort, independence, freedom, respect, love, and three-dollar panty hose that won't run."
—Phyllis Diller, as quoted in
Witty Words from Wise Women

To accurately determine what you can give to a negotiation, you need a place to start. Like a wise shopper who uses a grocery list to prevent emotional and impulse buys, you first must know exactly what it is you want. This sometimes means finding out what's possible.

Your simple answer may be, "I want a Mercedes at the best possible price." Or it may be, "I want this client to sign a $300,000 commercial lease." Those are goals. Those are your ultimate objectives.

A more complex and accurate answer might be, "I want the metallic blue Mercedes SLK 500 with payments I can easily afford and a guaranteed maintenance program from a dealer close to my house," or "I want this client to fall in love with the next place I show them, have impeccable credit, and no emotional baggage so they quickly and easily sign this $300,000 commercial lease."

In the charming film *Under the Tuscan Sun*, the heroine, Frances, wistfully wishes for a wedding in her own garden and a family to fill her large new villa. As the story progresses and loved ones and new friends fill her life, she gets her wish, although not exactly as she appeared to have wished it. But nonetheless, it is fulfilled.

We've all heard the phrase, "Be careful what you ask for—you just might get it." When it comes to negotiation, the need to be specific is doubly important. Without knowing your ultimate objective, it's impossible to know how to negotiate, or even accurately prepare for the negotiation.

> "The indispensable first step to getting the things you want out of life is this: decide what you want."
> —Ben Stein, *ThinkExist.com*

There are many layers to what you want. Perhaps you want that new Mercedes because it will be a symbol of all you've overcome to be able to get it. Perhaps you want it because your old BMW isn't running well anymore. Perhaps you believe that it will help you attract more clients, who will now perceive you as more successful.

The same with the $300,000 lease. You need the commission to pay your bills, to take a honeymoon cruise, because your kid needs braces, because you want to buy that gorgeous new house you saw last weekend.

No one wants things just for the things themselves. That goes for you and for the people with whom you negotiate. You don't want money for money's sake. Who needs little pieces of paper with pictures of dead people on them? You want what money can buy, and you want the feeling you will get from those purchases or investments.

If making the next deal is the only thing that matters in your world, for the sake of the deal alone, chances are you haven't got a lot of balance in your life with others. It also helps identify how and when to be flexible and creative.

Think about what the deal will do for you, how it will help you. What will it give you—tangibly and also in the feelings department. What's your motivation here? When you understand yourself, you can be more flexible.

Mercedes can't make the deal fit your wallet? Perhaps you'll go to Lexus or Jaguar.

The client prefers the smaller place you showed them two weeks ago? Perhaps their quickness at signing this deal for a place they love will allow you the time to make another deal happen.

You also need to understand the basics of the deal, too. In publishing we have what we call "deal points." These are specific things that are negotiable in every contract. They include things like the "Grant of Rights"—which rights the author is leasing to the publisher; the amount of money that will change hands and when; how big a piece of the revenues from the book the author will share in; when the book is due and how many pages; and many more things.

There are deal points in every industry. You will want to clearly understand the deal points possible for your contract/industry/negotiation. For a business negotiation, talk to five or six people who negotiate the same sort of contract. Ask them pertinent questions about the possibilities. What have they gotten that's creative, clever, smart, and helpful in their negotiations?

Literary agents share details like this among ourselves frequently. We learn what's possible from what other people were able to negotiate. Many times, there are numerous performance-related bonuses that cost nothing and yet motivate the author and publisher to sincerely promote the book aggressively. These are flexible, creative solutions I learned about and can now use. What can *you* learn?

In the case of a personal negotiation, for instance a home, there are many things you may not have thought of that can be negotiated in or out of the deal. How soon will escrow close? Will that be in time for you to close the house you live in now? Which furniture stays? Any appliances? How old are they? If you think the sofa goes perfectly with the living room carpet, will they leave it?

In the words of the wise Persian merchant, "Everything's negotiable."

Everything has a price, just about everything is for sale at the *right* price. If someone came to your door tonight and said, "I'll give you $4 million dollars for your home if you agree to move out by next Sunday night," what would you do? Other than calling the local geology department to find out if your house is sitting on a diamond mine, an oil well, or a vein of gold, you'd probably figure out a way to be out by next Sunday.

So what's your price? What do you really want here?

Write it down. Specifically write down the emotional goals, the tangible goals, and, exactly, in an ideal world, what you want. Then, you'll be able to logically judge how close you are to getting it.

People skip this step, but it's a critical one. It will show you where the "give room" is. If you insist on a four-bedroom, three-and-a-half-bath home, with 15 other amenities on the list, and you find a three-bedroom with everything else and a *den*, well, maybe you're flexible?

Without knowing what you want, you have no place to start. Once you know, you open the world to the possibility of fulfilling your desires.

> "Apparently there is nothing
> that cannot happen today."
> —Mark Twain, American author

Lucy Plyler works for a county in North Carolina, administering funds to public service programs. She and I were best friends in ninth grade, at a little parochial school in Prescott, Ariz. Lucy's family moved away, and in time, so did mine. We lost contact until she saw me one night on *Dateline NBC*, talking about one of my books. She tracked me down and we've been able to resume our friendship.

Lots of things have happened in both our lives. You probably have old school friends, too, and can look at how much has changed since the carefree days of giggling about boys and thinking about clothes and grades. Today, Lucy is the mother of three girls (who probably giggle like we did back then). Sadly, her youngest daughter has serious learning disabilities. Lucy's job for the county helped her develop keen negotiation skills, and she's been able to apply them to getting the help she needs with her daughter Heartleigh too. I asked her how she applies her skills to both tasks during one of our marathon catch-up phone calls.

She said, "In my child's education, I have to focus on what my special-needs child is supposed to get. I know what the state and the school system are supposed to do. Even though there are other things people are supposed to do, they don't always do them. In my job and personal life, I have to negotiate everything. That's just how it is.

"The most important part of negotiation is to let people know what you want. In dealing with other professionals in my job, I have to let them know what I want. It applies to my personal life, too.

"For example, my Heartleigh's education: early on we got the school system to pay for her to get a computer. We weren't sure if she could learn to talk and we knew what she needed, what we needed. But if we hadn't asked, we hadn't told them we wanted them to provide her with a computer, we wouldn't have gotten it. At work, when I let people know I need their data or certain things to make my job work and their job work, that's real important.

"And as a parent, I have to take care of myself and my child. I tried to stay calm when I was feeling like the teacher was unrealistic. I tried to figure out what's going on with me internally. Then I talked to some other people. I tried to discover if this was about me, or about the teacher. I don't want my child to get special treatment more than necessary, but I want her to get the help she needs.

"It turned out that I provided my daughter's teacher with a full diagnosis and a brief explanation summarizing what the doctors had said about my child. It was really successful because of the way my husband and I handled the meeting with the teacher. We offered her our partnership in our daughter's education. We approached her correctly and we were prepared and knew what we wanted. That helped a lot. She didn't have any reason for being defensive. I wasn't blaming her or anything. I didn't show any anger. Internally, I was conflicted about her and the situation, but I didn't show it. You have to act as allies, whether you're feeling it or not. You have to go above and beyond in some cases, over and over."

As we go through life, a clear understanding of what we want is the first place to start a negotiation of any kind. **The fourth principle of negotiation is knowing what you want and what's possible.** You may not get everything you want, but without a guidepost, you will never know if you've come close.

In another school negotiation example, Shirley Yuen describes the challenges she faced with her daughter's private school. Shirley is a professional speaker and parenting workshop leader, as well as author of an important book, *Three Virtues of Parenting* (Tuttle, 2004).

"I think negotiation gets down to what I truly believe in," Shirley explains. "You have to be sure exactly that you are negotiating what you want. I had some problems with my daughter's school last year. There was a big test. The teacher made a mistake. He gave my daughter a test that was missing one page. She got one page fewer than all the other students, because the teacher made a mistake. Then, this teacher kept refusing to give my daughter the test back. Maybe he was embarrassed at his mistake in not giving her all the pages. The report card came out and she got an F on the test. We asked to see the test, but couldn't. I wasn't asking to argue. If a parent requests to see her own child's test, unless you have something to hide, the test should be provided. They wanted her to repeat the whole course. She did and got an A. It's on her transcript now that she got an F. She had always been a straight-A student. So we have to explain everything. I was so upset.

"Sometimes, there are factors you cannot understand that are affecting the negotiation. In my daughter's case, it went deeper with the school. The things on the surface were not the things beneath it. There was unethical behavior behind the whole situation. That was the fuel for me. For me, negotiation gets down to just one thing: when I see something that is not just or ethical, I want justice and want the best outcome. I wanted it to turn out right. My questions weren't being answered. Things slowed down. I was making no progress.

"I saw something was not right behind the whole thing. I suspected a lot. Of course, next I had to do a lot of investigation. When you have to do so much research, you get to know the other parties very well. I wanted to know the facts: Who was running the school? Who was in the way? I asked why they weren't giving me what I wanted. I had to be honest with myself in the early stage and consider if I made a mistake in assuming they were doing something wrong when they weren't.

"Once I passed the stage of being angry, unreasonable, or impulsive, I saw that there really was injustice taking place.

"I had to analyze the whole situation to see the best way to negotiate. This large private school is a big power against a little person—me. They have a big board of directors. It is a very prestigious school. They just ignored me.

"They were protecting the teacher's mistake. If he would have admitted he made a mistake, I would have let the issue go. Instead, he blamed my daughter and tried to frame her as a bad student. I sent two or three letters of legal correspondence. They ignored me.

That was so very frustrating! When they stopped talking to me, it wasn't a negotiation anymore. When the ball is bouncing back and forth, that's a negotiation.

"One problem was that everyone I talked to on the board and in the school administration is male. I'm a minority female and was at a disadvantage. But I turned it around. In the end, it became an advantage to be a female, because I think we are more detail oriented—we look at the components. Women can determine how things affect each other. I always want to understand the root of the problem.

"It's so important to investigate. I had to go into the details behind the situation to understand exactly what happened, as Sherlock Holmes did. I had to put all the clues together, see if my daughter was giving me honest clues, find what was true, and what wasn't in what the school said. I did put them all together. I had to go to the school to gather all the details and choose which side I should believe (there are two sides to every story). If you are sure which side you are on, you have to know the weak and the strong points of your argument, especially if you are dealing with someone in power over you. You also have to realize he or she has weak points, too.

"The only way I could negotiate with the school was by getting help from other parents. I went through one phase of publicity already, to get other parents' support. I'm doing more publicity now, including the national news, letting them know it shouldn't be like this—they can do whatever they want to your kid.

"They now want to negotiate just to keep me quiet. Before, they wouldn't even answer me. That's when I had to think of another strategy.

"I couldn't fight a big school like this all alone. I hired two lawyers. Because I wanted to find out if there was any way I can pursue this legally, I asked the lawyer, 'Is there anything that protects the student from this sort of thing?' It turns out protection like this does not exist. Private schools are their own kingdom. Because this is wrong, I have two sponsors in the New Jersey Legislature now, and a bill coming up for a vote.

"I was very angry during this whole time. I was traumatized. I even had to go see a counselor. I was so upset it was hard to think straight. This is a trauma because they hurt my child. In negotiation if you don't have clarity, you can't see anything. By using the virtues I teach in my parenting book—Benevolence, Wisdom, and Courage—the Confucian virtues, you can handle any situation. Being angry is the opposite of benevolence, because you want to hurt someone. I had to get that under control, because I was very upset at what they had done to us.

"*Benevolence* is an act of kindness. In this case it was not for the school, but for the other students who might get damaged like my child was. When I decided I wanted to use that energy constructively, it helped me begin to stay calm. So much energy goes to the wrong things! You have to set your goal as benevolence. I want to put positive energy into what I want. I had to establish a goal, and it was justice. That stopped me from being angry. Don't let anger inside your thinking formula!

"Next comes *wisdom*. It's the path of wisdom to collect and then filter all the information, to put it all together in a way that helps you see the whole picture—a wise course of action. That way you ensure that you aren't biased. Wisdom helps you determine right and wrong. It helps you decide how to negotiate.

"Then it's time for *courage*. I asked myself *Do I have the courage to pursue and persist for a result I know I might never get* (the F being removed from her grade)? I said yes, and it has changed everything. It's given me a focus, and with this legislation that will pass, I believe it will help other parents and children not to have to suffer as we have."

Shirley Yuen made a point of "fact-collecting" in her negotiation and eventual attack on the policies of her daughter's former school. Probably the single most common factor in successful negotiation is something we all learned in school: the importance of doing our homework, our preparation. The next chapter talks all about preparation.

In Summary

Knowing precisely what you want and why you want it is the second most important skill to bring to a negotiation. Not only does it give you a place to start, it gives you bargaining room when the time comes for flexibility.

CHAPTER 8

The Importance of Being Ernest...or Betty or Lisa or Sue

"Men are taught to apologize for their weak-nesses, women for their strengths."
—Lois Wyse, as quoted in
Witty Words from Wise Women

Have you ever shaken hands with someone whose handshake is limp, puffy, and conveys only that they are either intimidated by you or by life?

Have you ever met—or are you—one of the women whose "little girl" voice never went away? Do telephone solicitors still ask you to put your mother on the phone?

Are you like my much-beloved friend Gayle, whom I lovingly call Snail? Snail, as she's been known since we were teens, is a soft, loving, kind-hearted, gentle woman. She apologizes for not calling me first every single time I call her. She cries at sad movies, hurt puppies, and bad news stories. She's an angel, but I'd never send her in to negotiate with a publisher for me or my clients.

Here's the truth: I don't think you can change a whole lot about your core personality if you're older than about 12 years old. Many Ph.D.s say who you are is pretty much set. Does that mean if you are a cocker spaniel instead of a pit bull, you're destined to a life of being taken advantage of?

Luckily, no. There are strengths to every personality style. Snail has an easier time of it because people trust and love her. They know she's good-hearted. People like me (my personality is basically the opposite of Snail's), trust me to get them a good deal, and "fight" for their rights. People don't mess with me because they are intimidated. People don't mess with Snail because she's such a nice person.

The trick is to love your lovely self. In order to love your self, you've got to know yourself and your own negotiation style. Once you know that, you can determine how to move through your life in ways that honor the precious Goddess energy you manifest and not spend your life wishing you were like someone else.

The universe is made up of positive and negative, sun and moon, up and down, salt and sweet. Neither is better, both are needed. Sometimes, we forget that we have all our power in the balance of the Earth. You probably know the Chinese symbol for this concept, called yin and yang—respectively representing (among other things) the feminine and the masculine energies. It is the image of a circle with the black swirl on one half, white on the other, each with an "eye" in the opposing color. The Earth needs both the masculine and feminine for balance. Each woman contains a touch of masculinity that she can draw upon. Each man has a touch of femininity. There's no disharmony in that, no dishonor in using the gift of our gender with its garnish of the opposite.

We have a privilege in learning who we are, embracing our unique mix of more ying or more yang. In order to love ourselves and build strong negotiations from the depths of our inherent characters, we need to understand which we are. The simple, fun test on page 59 will help you figure yourself out even better. And the better you know yourself, the more you can come from your strengths.

> "You negotiate differently depending on who the players are and what your field is. There are guidelines but if they are counter-intuitive to your personality, you will come across as insincere. You have to adapt and adopt them to your personal style to make them work."
> —Bonnie Paul,
> corporate interior design expert

Know Thyself

Bottom line: it's time for some playful self-analysis. This handy little quiz will help you determine if you are more *yin*, feminine, or *yang*, masculine, and perhaps give you some room to balance, at least temporarily, when you are in a negotiation situation. Just circle T (True) or F (False) to describe what's true, or mostly true, for you.

Do-It-Yourself Yin-Yang Quiz:
Discover Your Personal Negotiation Style

1. I own more pink clothes than any other color.   T or F

2. I have fluttered my eyelashes at a male in the last 12 months to encourage him to do something for me.   T or F

3. It is an insult to how far we've come as women to even ask such stupid questions as question 1 and 2. Gender is not relevant in negotiation situations between professionals.   T or F

4. I like to be seen as really pretty and soft.   T or F

5. If I could choose a female mentor, I'd probably choose Gloria Allred.   T or F

6. If I could choose a female mentor, I'd probably choose Goldie Hawn.   T or F

7. Most people are a little afraid of me.   T or F

8. I like to be seen as very smart and professional.   T or F

9. I'd like to be treated differently at work and in negotiations.   T or F

10. People bring me their problems, because I listen and care.   T or F

11. I usually present myself to the people with whom I work as being too busy for frivolity, very focused, and extremely self-assured.   T or F

12. I don't really think much about how the people I work with see me. I am pretty much "one of the gang."   T or F

13. I tend to fall in the middle, sometimes very feminine, sometimes more masculine. I adapt to the situation at hand.   T or F

14. When the job needs doing, I'm the one who gets it done. I consider myself not only competent, but versatile.   T or F

Results

If you answered True to all or most of the questions numbered 1, 2, 4, 6, 10, and 12, chances are you are very in touch with your feminine side. You are more "yin." But if you also answered True to question 9, then you certainly will benefit from learning and applying the lessons in this book.

If you answered True to all or most of the questions numbered 3, 5, 7, and 11, chances are you have learned to be very in touch with your masculine or "yang" side. But if you also answered True to question 9, then you certainly will benefit from learning and applying the lessons in this book.

Questions 8, 13, and 14 represent the goal we have for when you finish reading this book. The smartest women know that being able to use all the skills at their disposal to get the job done to the best of their abilities is the name of the game, especially in negotiations. Being adaptable, versatile, and able to fluidly move from one presentation or personality style to another doesn't mean you have a personality disorder—it means you have learned to love your whole self, honor all your gifts, recognize the value of the skills inherent to non-dominant side, and are also able to use them to support you in your goals.

CHAPTER 9

The Power of Preparation

"Initiative means one thing to star performers and quite another to the middle performers. One middle performer told of gathering and organizing source materials, including documents and software tools, for a project he was beginning with his group. Another described writing a memo to his superior about a software bug. Both thought they were showing initiative. But star performers regarded these as routine actions. Of course you fix a software bug when you find it. Of course you prepare in advance for a project. So what else is new? To the stars, initiative involves creative actions that go beyond the routine."

—Nido Qubein, author of
Achieving Peak Performance

Imagine you have decided to throw a little dinner party for six people this Friday. You've remembered to invite your guests, but Friday afternoon while at work, it suddenly hits you: people are coming and your house is a mess! You have done nothing to prepare! There's nothing to eat in the entire place except a tired frozen pot pie living a lonely life in the freezer, a half-wilted head of lettuce, and a half a dozen eggs.

Being a modern woman, you will quickly call a take-out place you trust, leave work early to tidy up a bit, and pray to God no one shows up early. You may be able to pull it off, but how relaxed will you be? Will you look on that party with fond memories? Or will you spend the time hoping no guest accidentally opens the broom closet, where you have stored pretty much everything you scooped up that was on the floor three hours ago…and where *is* the dog?

Wouldn't it have been better to have been prepared? You could have bought the food in advance, cooked in advance whatever can handle preparation early, dropped Fido off at the groomer's on Thursday morning, made sure the cleaning lady came on Thursday, and only had to tidy up a few random morning-rush leftovers on Friday after work. You would have picked up fresh flowers on your way home, had time to make place cards in calligraphy that would make Martha Stewart proud of you. What if you had set the table Thursday evening while watching *Seinfeld* re-runs and then tossed a sheet over it to keep off the dust?

Wouldn't you have had a much more relaxing evening? Of course you would have.

Preparation is the key to pretty much *everything.* When I was much younger, in my mid-20s, I owned my fourth business, a tiny catering company. I learned first hand the incredible important of advance preparation when it comes to parties, food and social events.

Preparation and planning go hand in hand. Your job as a good negotiator, now that you've accomplished the first critical steps, is to grab onto the **fifth principle of negotiation: Be prepared.**

Bonnie Paul, Philadelphia Regional President of the National Association of Women Business Owners (NAWBO), 1991-1993, and a very successful art dealer, teaches us, "The strength is doing your homework, knowing those to whom you are talking as best you can. The weakness is underestimating someone else.

"You have to know what goals you are trying to achieve, know the other party's hot buttons, and know how to push them. That takes preparation. An attorney doesn't ask a question unless he knows the answer. I always want to know, 'Have they collected certain types of art in the past?' 'Where are they headed?' I don't ever want to go into anything blindly.

"I join organizations and build up relationships with people who can tell me about a specific client's background. This has helped me to know how to approach each person. I think we all have to learn how to ask key questions in a non-confrontational way.

"I find that, generally, artists can be very naïve and can be easily led. I try to be their advocate. They can get taken advantage of in a deal. But I'm their middle man. I take care of my artists without penalizing my clients. I pay very quickly and use this as leverage. This way, I have an excellent relationship with my artists all the time, and they trust me and want to work with me again.

"I take all the things—all aspects of everyone's needs and wants—into consideration when I go into a negotiation. I am sensitive to both sides' needs and I want to come out with a win-win result. Sometimes the whole money issue has to get out of the way. It's better to make something than nothing. It's not going to be published in a national newspaper that you sold some art at a discount. What someone can get for a piece depends on the economy and so many other things. If you know the client wants something and the offer is reasonable, I always say take it. Get it going. Maybe someone will want more, or someone will see the painting and want one of their own.

"The most successful negotiation I ever did took eight months to a year to complete. It was a $1 million painting. The artist's widow had it and she didn't want to let it go. It was a truly premier piece by the artist. We had to continually woo her and assure her that this painting was going to be respected and honored. Her terms were that it had to be lent to a certain museum for a certain period of time every year. She needed to be sure it was going to be shown and respected, and it made the client look good because it went to the museum. It was a gradual acceptance for the widow, a gradual trust being built by her in us. That was important for everyone. And everyone won."

She Who Is Most Prepared, Wins

If you are entering into a negotiation with someone, wouldn't you want to know the most about them and the deal points as you possibly can?

A woman we'll call Lori sells average cars in Santa Monica, Calif., where I have my offices. One day, I asked her if she likes selling luxury cars or average cars more (she's done both). She laughed. Then she gives me this incredible insight:

"When I sold for a luxury car dealer, I was interacting with a different type of buyer. These buyers, these people, are smart. They come into the dealership fully prepared. They know which options cost what, what we pay for the car, what our markup is, and sometimes even things such as how long it has been on the lot! They look at the mileage and know what's been sitting. The buyers for luxury cars know what they're talking about. So there's really almost no selling to it. You just work out the numbers if you can and they take it or they don't. In that role, I'm more of an order taker. But the profits are really, really small because those people carve it down to the last penny.

"With average cars, Camrys and Accords and the like, the buyers are rarely prepared. They often have issues like bad credit or unreasonable expectations because they don't understand the business of cars. They either ask for too much or they take bad deals gladly because they just don't know any better. I get to use my selling skills more, but I deal with people who are not as enjoyable as customers. I make more money selling them, though, because they'll sign a deal that's more in the dealership's favor and won't even know it."

From our perspectives as car buyers, this is an enlightening story. I'll bet that Lori isn't far different from any other car salesperson anywhere. If you could get car dealers to tell it to you straight, they'd all say some version of the same thing: the better cars go to the better-prepared customers. Could it be that these better-prepared customers can afford the luxury cars because they apply that same level of professionalism and preparation to other factors in their lives, too?

While on the most obvious level, this true story is proof that we should all get on the Internet and do some checking before we go car shopping. At a deeper level, it is a testament to the power of preparation.

Imagine going into court without any evidence. Crazy!

Imagine accusing your spouse of infidelity without a whisper of evidence. Crazy!

Imagine hiring an employee without checking references. Crazy!

Failure to plan
is planning to fail.
—Unknown

Your single greatest responsibility in making sure a negotiation goes your way is to put preparation time into it.

You probably take a grocery list to the store with you. Assuming you don't also take your kids, you probably purchase most of what's on the list. Your shopping trip to get what you want is pretty stream-lined. It's easier to get what you want and need when you take the list, which is probably why you make a list each time you shop. Here's an important checklist to help you prepare for negotiations ahead of time. Make sure you have all these items for a successful negotiation.

Successful Negotiation Checklist

- What the other party needs and wants, on the surface and below.
- That the person you are negotiating with has final approval power.
- What leverage you have on them.
- What you absolutely must have to make the deal make sense.
- What latitude you have for maneuvering.
- What it will take to close the negotiation favorably.
- What is driving the other party to negotiate with you in the first place.
- How to shift the power in your favor.

Only when you have thoroughly prepared yourself are you ready to negotiate.

This preparation may be instant, as in, "Johnny, if you don't eat the spinach, you won't get any dessert." In that case, where you have complete control of dessert and therefore complete leverage, you win 9 times out of 10.

Other preparation may be lengthy, as in trying to prove fault in a legal case, but it is critical to your success in any negotiation. So why don't more women do it?

Time Out of Mind

Preparation is skipped by women for one factor: time.

Most women reading this book probably have kids. There's half your time right there. I'm a single working mother, so I have less time than I'd like to prepare for anything. Women are starting to realize equality is not like winning the lottery. We all didn't suddenly get butlers, chauffeurs, and nannies. Mostly, we got to be bread-winners *and* moms *and* home managers. It's balancing it all that drains most of our time and it is the lack of time that makes us unlikely to put in the extraordinary effort to be 100 percent prepared and organized in a negotiation, or even to apply the creativity to think up unique win-win solutions or butter up our negotiation partners.

If you're one of the millions of women who readily blame "lack of time" for not being more prepared, I can only say I understand...and I have a solution.

Think back, if you will, to the "Terrible Twos." Remember your child's sudden ability to break, drop, spill, and plunder everything, simultaneously, from morning until night?

Perhaps you'd rather not go back down memory lane, but you learned a skill during that period that will help you now. Remember some parenting advice you got from a friend or a book? What was it? It was, "Pick your battles." We've mentioned that before. The other part is, "Let the rest go."

Okay, so you don't have time to really thoroughly research which carpet installation company is going to give you the absolute rock-bottom best price for the best carpet? Let it go. Spend your time nego-tiating bigger things, such as the promotion you're up for at work.

A business mentor once told me, "If you can make $100 per hour doing what you do at work, then never do anything anywhere, any time, for which someone else could be paid less than $100 to perform it."

Prepare for the things that are critically important to you and your future. Let slide the things that are not. I know a man who sells sub-scriptions to a weekly delivery of boxed food to busy families. Every week, a truck comes and brings them groceries. At first, I couldn't imagine such a service existed. I like picking out my own vegetables, thank you.

Upon reflection, the 60 minutes I spend in the two grocery stores I patronize every week could be put to better use, even if it's just taking a well-deserved nap. Not to mention writing a book or helping my clients market their speaking or books.

It's all coming down to matters of time. Pick the things you will research. If $100 is a lot of money to you, then any time you need to negotiate in a matter that is worth $100 or more to you, put the time into preparing the negotiation materials you need. If the number is $500 or $1,000 or $100,000, then put the time in there.

Logically, you cannot prepare in depth for every negotiation. You cannot pursue every opportunity with equal gusto—at least not for long. Choose your battles, and give yourself a break. And if you want the phone number of the food subscription guy, send me an e-mail!

In Summary

Preparation is the single most important factor in determining your success as a negotiator. It pays off—find the time!

CHAPTER 10

Applied Preparation

> "There are any number of life situations for which preparation is necessary. Negotiation is one of these. For successful results, it requires...preparation and training."
> —Gerard I. Nierenberg,
> *The Complete Negotiator*

Okay, you acknowledge that preparation is critical. But where does one begin to gather all the facts? You're not Columbo or Magnum PI, although hiring someone like them might not be a bad idea.

In California, we have a huge problem with fraudulent worker's compensation claims. I knew a man who ran a "sub rosa" company. I had not heard the term. He turned out to be an investigator. His team would follow someone claiming back injury to the local cowboy bar and get photos of him doing the two-step and then dipping his partner. His men would "stake out" houses where the homeowners were using their disability time and money to renovate the home.

That's formal and expensive investigation. In a legal matter, of course you would do this preparation for a very formal and expensive negotiation (called a trial).

On a lesser note, my neighbor has two Jack Russell terriers. These dogs are insane. Not only is yapping their only pastime while locked out for days at a time on my neighbor's porch, but she lets them out to run the neighborhood at least once a day. Invariably, they come to my house to harass my fenced-in German Shepherd/Lab mix, Lucky. Lucky hates these dogs on his property, so he snarls. They snarl. A growling match ensues every night between 9 p.m. and 11 p.m. Last month, one of these wretched pests found a new hole in the fence—or dug one—and got into our yard. In a fight with Lucky, the Jack Russell tore off a big part of my dog's ear! At last, my seven months of photographing these pests in my yard and recording the dates of their offences are coming in handy. We have a court date already set for this month.

That's far less preparation for a far less expensive negotiation. At the simplest level, an applicant for a job hoping to land the position would take 15 minutes to peruse the Website of her prospective employer if she wants the job, so she can talk knowledgeably about the company to which she is applying.

The amount of preparation required is determined by the reward at stake for the preparation. Dashing off a list of things to remember to discuss with your housemate takes a few seconds, but compiling data about the company to which you hope to sell a $25,000 technology solution will take considerably more time. The following examples will help you plan your preparation strategy effectively.

Preparation Pays Off:
A Business-to-Business Example

Whether you are negotiating in a business situation or in a personal one, preparation will be critical to how well the negotiation goes. The following is a business-to-business (B2B) example:

Jeanne Coughlin, author of *The Rise of Female Enterpreneurs* (Quorum Books, 2002), gives this helpful example:

"I was moving into a role as chairman of one of the largest small-business associations in Cleveland. We were going through master contract negotiations with our healthcare insurance provider. This was a multimillion dollar contract.

"We had a whole team of people negotiating this deal. Team negotiations are easier because someone can play bad cop and the other good cop.

"Now, I'm not a believer in using tirades in negotiating, but the actuary or the attorney can approach the deal from some aspects that I cannot. You don't want people to be guarded or formal. You want to be able to ask people what they are thinking and get straight answers. What Columbo did was disarm people and then make them think he was a bumbling fool and then sneak in a real important question at the end. I think asking general 'dumb questions' helps sometimes.

"So in our first meeting, the insurance provider extended an offer in which we weren't interested. I was the only woman in that meeting. I had asked an open-ended question to get the conversation flowing. I asked why they wanted us to accept that proposal, why they wanted us to sign a more expensive contract.

"They were candid in their response. They said, 'We need to make more money on your program.' That meant we were at opposite ends of the spectrum. Our goal was to save small business owners money. So my approach to this, as with any negotiation, was, 'Let's find where we have common ground and work from there.' The situation got a little bit contentious. My first priority became to establish a personal relationship with everyone in the situation so that they were relaxed and friendly, and therefore open to seeing more than just their perspective.

"The bigger the deal is, the more important relationship is. People ultimately communicate with people. The more you understand about the other person, the better the deal is going to be.

"A big point for me in all my negotiations is that you have to enter into the process having as many facts as you can. It's true that negotiators are trained to play games and not get angry and not get swept up in the emotion. You have to know all the facts from your side and as many as you can gather from the other side. The more prepared you are, the quicker you will know when you have reached that middle point or if you are being unreasonable. You must know what they are trying to accomplish and what's driving them."

Remember:

- ❧ Preparation is critical.
- ❧ People negotiate more easily with people they like and trust.
- ❧ Knowing your parameters and theirs is critical.
- ❧ Keeping levelheaded and aware of all elements of the negotiation is invaluable.

So in a B2B negotiation, for what questions do you dig up the answers (which answers might have value for you)? And where can you find these answers?

You'd be surprised how easy it is. You can get so much information about a company and its principals from the Internet. Another tactic is to call someone's secretary. Make a pal out of her over the phone. Ask how things are going. Go to the place of business, without identifying yourself. Listen in on how the employees are talking about the company in the lobby or lunchroom. Talk to the guard at the desk or the janitor. Ask questions of the people who really know the state of the company's health.

Fact Gathering

In addition to talking to people who work for the company, you can collect facts on a company by reading the newspaper of the city in which it is housed. As mentioned previously, you can get this information on the Internet as well. Take time to carefully and thoroughly review the company's Website. Check to find out what its industry magazine is and see if it's been featured in it, or is well known in its industry. See if the industry is suffering. See if the company's region or its product is being beaten by a competitor.

If you had been in charge of IT for your company, and you decided to invest in Macintosh computers for the whole office's word-processing needs, you would have quickly found yourself in trouble. With a little research, you could have seen the writing on the wall—that PCs would "win" the battle.

Companies don't acquire problems overnight. They tend to build gradually. In most cases, the larger the company, the more public its problems are. You will want to find out as much as you can about the company before you enter negotiations.

The easiest, fastest, most effective ways to do your sleuthing are:

🐾 Read newspapers and magazines.

🐾 Talk to employees.

🐾 Visit the facility.

🐾 Check Dun & Bradstreet (D&B), *Consumer Reports,* and so on.

🐾 Check any other rating systems available.

🐾 Read the company's Website.

🐾 Talk to its disgruntled and its happy customers.

🐾 Get a "feel" for the company by spending 15 minutes waiting in the lobby before your appointment.

🐾 Find out how its industry is doing.

🐾 Compare prices, service, and terms of its competition.

🐾 Talk to other businesspeople who have used or not used the company and find out why.

🐾 Don't let the company's advertising copy "sell" you—do your homework.

When you are buying a service, it's important to think rationally about what options you have. If you are buying commercial janitorial services, for instance, there are enough purveyors that it doesn't matter much which one you pick. You'll just find one that offers the best service at the best price and be done with it. The only negotiation is how much cheaper you can get it if you agree to the service for longer, or less often, or cut out some of the services, and so on. Because some purveyors such as carpet cleaners, long distance carriers, and cell phone companies are so prevalent, you, the customer, have all the power. It's a "buyer's market."

But if you are trying to get a good deal on plutonium chips to run your nuclear submarine (or whatever runs submarines) there probably aren't too many purveyors. You need them way more than they need you, and, as a result, your goal is to determine your ultimate bottom line—what you are willing to pay and on what the terms. They have more leverage than you do. For instance, they may want payment in small, unmarked bills in a black attaché case at midnight. You might only have a navy blue Gucci handbag to offer.

Luckily, most negotiations come somewhere in between janitorial and criminal. In most cases, determining in advance who has leverage and who thinks they have leverage and why they do gives you the advantage.

Preparation Pays Off: A Business-to-Consumer Example

Whether you're buying a car, a washing machine, or any item that seems too expensive, preparation pays off. You already "comparison shop" as part of your daily life and may not realize it.

Who would hire a contractor to remodel their bathroom without getting ideas and quotes from several, and checking the references of each?

If you found that your grocery store consistently charged 20 percent more for items you buy every week, wouldn't you shop elsewhere?

Comparison shopping for food and contractors is a skill that applies to any business-to-consumer transaction (B2C).

A female friend told me she was shopping for a new car. She said "I'm really bad at negotiations for stuff outside of my work. What I found worked for me was having material—paper—in my hands. I went to the manufacturer's Website, found out the price of the car, and then I went to the *Blue Book*. I had never done this! It was easy. I walked into the dealership and put the papers on his desk. I said 'This is the car I want, the price I want, and these are the conditions and features I want.'

"This was the only thing I could do, because I'm not good at negotiations. Guess what? It worked. I got the car at the price I wanted."

I recommend using the Rule of Three. It can save you lots of money and heartache throughout your life. Three takes little effort. It will be worth it.

The Rule of Three

Get three bids, three prices, three retailers, three salespeople, and/or three opinions on the quality of anything BEFORE you buy. Shop in three stores before making a decision. You may not always want the cheapest, you may not always want the most expensive, but your risk factor goes way down if you select the middle price.

How to Research a Major Personal Purchase

If you are buying a thing—a car, an appliance, anything you see as expensive—you have a chance to negotiate. Even if it has a price tag, there's often room for negotiation. Like the time you found the perfect sweater, but it needed dry cleaning because someone had tried it on with pink lipstick. Remember how you got the store manager to mark it down 10 or 20 percent?

There are all sorts of factors that go into your bigger negotiations, depending on what you want. Price is just a part of it. If Store A told you can get you a brand new, name-brand washing machine for 75 percent less than any of its competition, but that it came from the manufacturer in another country and it will take four months to arrive by banana boat, would you agree to buy it?

Yes, if you can wait four months to wash clothes or you have an alternative, such as a Laundromat nearby.

If you can't wait, the answer will be no. It's that simple.

We're Not Best Buy

I recently bought an expensive piece of electronics for my computers at work. I asked the Office Depot salesman about their return policy on opened packages. I wanted to know what happened if it turned out that I was buying the wrong piece of equipment. I hadn't prepared for this because I didn't know DSL came in different speeds, and I certainly didn't know which speed of DSL we have. I wanted to get it over with right now, I didn't want to buy both of them to find out which one worked and then have to come back to return one.

He said, "Just bring it back."

I said, "What if it's opened? I have to install it to determine if it's the right one. What's the restocking fee?"

He said, "Bring it back. No restocking fee. We're not Best Buy."

I bought it there, right then. Best Buy had been my very next destination to see if I could get it $10 to $20 cheaper. The price was worth it to me because of the return policy.

There are many other elements to negotiation. The following questions will arm you with the information you need and the questions to ask when you go into a store or place of business to buy an item.

Personal Purchase Questions

1. Is it the best price? Can I afford it easily?

2. If the company/store offers a payment plan and I need to use it, is the interest less than my credit card charges— or more?

3. If I use a payment plan, am I 100-percent certain I can pay it off before they start sticking me with insane interest rates? (PS: That's how places of business make a lot of money—most customers don't have the money later on.)

4. If I take part in the payment plan, can the interest not begin until X date, and not accrue in the meantime if I don't pay it off on that precise day?

5. Can it be delivered? When? For how much? Why isn't it free?

6. Do they haul away my old one?

7. What's the guarantee? The warranty? (They are different words!)

8. Does the product have all the features I need?

9. Is it the right color, size, shape?

10. What did the company/store pay to stock it? (Look on the Internet.)

11. How much is the salesperson's commission?

12. What's the store's standard employee discount? (Hint: You can get this info by calling the personnel department. The percentage represents the smallest discount you should get on the item.)

13. Can I buy it used cheaper? (eBay? Damark.com? Newspaper? Other?)

14. Is it in stock? If I have to wait, can I have a discount?

15. Is it "Made in America" (if that's important to you)?

16. Does the company have damaged/reconditioned ones anywhere? How much would I save if I bought one of those? And how long is the warranty or guarantee on those? (Often much longer!)

17. Is the salesperson hungry? (Hint: "So, how's business been, Jim?")

18. Is the manager or owner panicky over revenues? (Hint: An independent store running huge sales is trying to liquidate inventory to either move, cash out, close, or file for bankruptcy.)

19. Is the store crowded? If it is, chances are the products sold there are priced well below their perceived values.

20. Can I return it, only exchange it, or neither?

21. What is the exact process to follow for the warranty? Do I have to ship it to Taiwan myself and hope it comes back someday repaired?

22. Does the store offer support to help me if it malfunctions? If so, is it on the phone or in person? Will someone be sent to my house? (Hint: If it's by phone, call as if you had a technical problem and see how long the wait time is—*before* you buy.)

23. Is the lowest price garunteed? For how long? (Hint: Stores readily do this because human nature dictates that once

you've bought the item you seek, you stop watching the ads for it because your need is satisfied.)

24. How long can I wait to own it?

You may not realize...

ᐬ American consumers, unlike people in other countries, have been trained to sheepishly pay whatever the sticker price or salesperson says. This is an outrage!

ᐬ Jewelry is often marked up 200 percent, 300 percent, or more!

ᐬ Competition for your dollar is so fierce in most industries any small business is starving for your patronage!

ᐬ "Big box" stores often have managers who will give you discount if you take something that was already opened or somehow damaged in the store.

ᐬ Liquidators, the Internet, and discount stores such as Ross, Marshalls, T.J. Maxx, and Big Lots often have merchandise *identical* to the more expensive stores, at much lower prices. This has changed the state of American business. As a consumer, you have the power to negotiate the price on anything! You may not *always* get your wish, but you will get it more often than you think. You can hand them your money, or you can negotiate. It's easy, and it's your choice.

You need to also ask *yourself* two starkly honest questions. These are the ones we don't want to ask when we're longing for that cute new pair of shoes.

1. How badly do I need it? (Hint: We're far more likely to buy what we want than what we need, hence huge consumer debt. Can you wait for it? How long?)

2. Is it exactly what I like, or will I always want something else? (A wise older woman told me, when I was a newlywed, "Never buy anything you think you can make do with until you can get something better. See that lamp over there? I bought that 20 years ago and am still making do. I've hated it for 20 years.")

Damaged Goods! Big Sale!

Two brothers I know used to own an appliance shop. Four times a year, they'd have a damaged merchandise sale. The price of anything that got damaged on the floor, in transport, or in the warehouse was marked way down. The store was always packed during their sales. People couldn't believe they could get $100 off just because the back of the fridge was scratched or dented a bit, where no one would see it anyway. But the well-trained salespeople were quick to point out "rich people only buy perfect goods." What they didn't mention is that in back, in the warehouse, a couple of guys with mallets and razor blades were creating "damaged goods" as fast as customers could buy them.

Always ask for the damaged goods discount. Maybe they can "find" you something in the back room to make the sale.

In every negotiation, the more prepared you are, the more armed with facts, figures, dates, statistics, and thorough knowledge (of what you want and what's possible) you are, the more prepared you are to win.

In Summary

Preparation stacks the odds in your favor, especially because most people fail to prepare thoroughly.

CHAPTER 11

How to Prepare in a Personal Situation

> "Preparation calls into operation a simple and obvious rule of physics: Unless there is something in the reservoir, nothing can flow from it. 'Nothing in, nothing out,' as computer people say."
>
> —Gerry Spence,
> *How To Argue and Win Every Time*

As emphasized in the story told earlier by Shirley Yuen of the lengths to which she went in order to determine why her bright daughter suddenly got an F on a test, preparation for a personal negotiation is often part of a woman's life.

Michele Weldon in her best-selling book for women in difficult marriages, *I Closed My Eyes* (Hazelden, 1999), talks about preparing for a divorce by collecting dates and times of abuse occurrences. In the case of my neighbor's psychotic Jack Russells, the issue of dates and photographs is critically important to my case.

If you are ever in the situation where you are building a case, it's wise to keep records. If you are planning on bringing incomplete chores to your child's attention, or showing the trash company managers that the men who pick up your trash scatter it all over your yard, or dealing with an unfaithful spouse, you will need to compile evidence to prove your case.

This means actually keeping a log of events. In the case of a teen-ager who just won't feed the dog or pick up his or her room, you can scream until you are blue in the face without yielding results and he or she will still believe you owe him or her an allowance. But by keeping a log of the days, making it clear that you are doing so, and clearly stating the contingencies if the room is not kept clean you are far more likely to help yourself win the negotiation.

My mom used the "Garbage Bag" threat quite effectively as a negotiation tool in this matter. If my room wasn't clean by a certain time, anything left on the floor would be confiscated, dropped in a large plastic bag, and kept away from me for a predetermined period of time. It was a highly effective negotiation tactic, made so because she had the power to enforce it.

Along with your log of dates and times, you may need visual evidence to support your case. A famous Florida divorce attorney I represented in negotiation said that more parents would win custody battles if they took the time to record every single instance when the other parents blew off a date with the children, was late, or was rude.

In preparation for personal negotiations, sometimes you have to think outside the box. For example, to find out if your child is a trouble-maker at school, you may have to call the counselor, a few teachers, and the principal and then have a casual chat with some of his friends.

To find out if a neighboring property owner is definitely planning to cut down a tree on the property line between your homes, despite reassurances that it is not so, you may need to go to the plans department to see if the proposed new house requires the tree be removed.

You need to ask yourself a few questions as you prepare for personal situations:

- ♣ Who has the information I do not have?
- ♣ How can I get them to give it to me?
- ♣ Am I keeping track (on paper) of names, dates, times, events?
- ♣ Can I provide objective physical proof (photos, notes from the teacher, arrest warrants, parking tickets, dog poop by your flower bed from a dog that isn't yours, and so forth)?

- ♣ Is there a verifiable third party who can second my opinion? (For example, my other neighbor is also terrorized by the Jack Russells.)
- ♣ Can I get someone else to hand me the information I seek?

The Clever Ruse

I met a handsome single businessman in 1996 toward whom I felt an instant and undeniable attraction. Apparently, it was mutual. We sat in a restaurant and talked until 3 a.m. Mesmerized and thinking this is what is meant by love at first sight, I had a hard time tearing myself away to go home.

The next morning he woke me up with a phone call. I knew he lived in Chicago and that he was flying to Portland that morning to his next appointment. He said he'd called to tell me how wonderful and beautiful I was. What a way to wake up! He said he couldn't wait to see me again when he returned to Los Angeles next week. We set a date. He promised to call when he got to his hotel in Portland.

Excited, happy, delighted, I counted my amazing good fortune and fell back asleep. That afternoon, flowers arrived! Sure enough, I got a long, tender phone call that evening. I was charmed. How had I gotten so lucky?

The next day, nothing. And nothing the day after that, and the day after that, and the day after that. I left him two messages on his cell phone in five days. Nothing. I began to fear he'd been hurt. Slowly, I panicked that this wonderful, ephemeral romance had disappeared before it got far. I pondered what to do. I needed more facts.

On a sudden hunch, I called his office, claiming I was "Susan from Dr. Albright's office" and that we were trying to send David and his wife a Christmas gift. "Could I please have the spelling of his wife's name?"

Without a moment's hesitation, she spelled out the name "Julie." I had been tricked! Of course I was hurt and sad, but by calling the office, I was able to get some information that helped me make better choices. Sometimes, simply a phone call from you or your alter ego can help you gather up information that will help you in negotiations or in life.

Armed With Truth

When it comes to matters of our personal lives, preparing for the showdown can be painful to the point of trauma, depending on the magnitude of the issue. But the more painful the negotiation will be, the more important it is that you have thorough and accurate data.

It barely needs saying that a spouse's infidelity is often uncovered by the proverbial note left in a jacket pocket. Psychologists claim that at such instances, the discovered party actually could bear the suspense of duplicity no more and subconsciously was careless. It is the unspoken, unmentionable accusations that disrupt most interpersonal relationships.

I'm going to share a story of which I am ashamed, but it will help you as you prepare for the negotiations in your personal life. As you read, remember: facts—hard, tangible facts—would have dissipated assumptions and saved a very important relationship in my life.

Sharon's Story

In 1991, I was in very serious car accident in which two people I loved very much were killed. I was horribly injured (if you'd like to know more, or are dealing with your own loss, bereavement, or chronic pain, please go to *www.Lifepresent.org*). As I went through the agonizing recovery process, my friend Sharon Gibbs became my constant companion. She was a dear source of comfort and strength. She took time from her own work at the Alhambra, Calif., Chamber of Commerce to drive the 40 minutes to my house several times a week.

I'm not sure I could have survived were it not for her kindness and listening skills. I told her everything I was thinking and feeling. I trusted her implicitly.

In 1994, it became apparent that the effects of the accident had driven a silver spike through the heart of my 10-year marriage. My husband moved out, and I stayed in our home with my daughter.

To keep myself sane, I wrote often in my journal. I wrote deep personal things. Things I would never tell anyone, except Sharon. Somehow, my ex-husband knew the things I was writing in my secret journal. At first, I couldn't understand how he knew these things. Perhaps Sharon was telling her husband, who was then telling mine.

Again and again it happened. Things he should not have found out, things that made the painful divorce process all the more agonizing. Sharon could be the only leak. I was devastated at her betrayal. I confronted her on it, angrily accusing her of feeding my information to her husband, or of secretly telling him herself.

She and I instantly stopped talking—forever. But he kept finding out my secrets. Until I had a security system installed that prevented him from pulling a window off its track in the back bedroom, climbing in, reading my journal, and then replacing it between the mattress where I kept it hidden.

If I had been prepared for what was really a negotiation with Sharon, I would have considered alternatives to her being the "leak" in my system. I would have been creative in ways to solve this problem. I would not have sacrificed a true friend for the sake of poor preparation.

In Summary

Get the facts! Get the right facts from credible sources, assemble them carefully, get verified documentation, and *then* proceed with your negotiation.

CHAPTER 12

Preparing Your Self for Success

"You've got to take the initiative and play
your game. In a decisive set,
confidence is the difference."
—Chris Evert, Tennis Pro

The only thing that will be the same in all your negotiations will be you. You are the only common denominator. Learning to be the best negotiator you can be is a matter of collecting the skills, the information, and the confidence you need to make it easy for you to get the terms you want with minimum resistance.

The following section will teach you to walk, talk, look, and act the part of a woman who knows what she wants and is used to getting it. Your confidence will surge when you apply these basic principles to your negotiation skills. Confidence and its sister expectation are important factors of how successful a negotiation will be.

Power of Confidence

Susan Nicolas is one of the most successful saleswomen of a line of well-known jewelry and scarves in the country. She sells to all the swanky shops in resorts in her territory. Her effervescence and great attitude are apparent every time she walks into a store.

Imagine her life: She gets up in the morning, drives to a small boutique in a resort town somewhere, and pitches her lines of merchandise. Frequently, she knows the owners; sometimes the place is under new management. Sometimes, she probably doesn't feel like walking in. Often, the shop owners are probably busy, tired, distracted, or annoyed to see yet another salesperson walking in.

You think you've got a tough job? But Susan is one of the highest revenue producing people in her industry. Here's what she says about attitude:

"I automatically turned on the confidence. Like a switch. I tell the people, 'Okay, this is what we're going to do,' instead of asking permission. When I know what I'm selling is the best, I automatically assume the person is going to buy it. It's not a yes/no close. There is no true no. They're crazy if they don't buy! It got to the point once when I was selling something so hot, I would walk in and say, 'Why don't you just take money out of your pocket right now and throw it away, because that's what you're doing by not carrying this product.'"

Susan had leverage, confidence, and a clever, powerful close. No wonder she gets such a high percentage of reorders. If you believe what you're negotiating for is right, good, and just, you have no reason to back down.

"A powerful woman knows how powerfully she affects the world around her. A powerful woman owns her part."
—Marilyn Graman and Maureen Walsh,
The Female Power Within

Susan exudes confidence, and her clients respond to it. She says, "I prayed today, as I was walking through my house. I prayed to God because I hadn't gotten any orders. I prayed and I just got two days worth of orders! God told me a long time ago He'd take care of me. Do you know that scripture about how the birds don't worry about eating and He clothes the lilies of the valley? It's a matter of trust, skill, the cycle of things.

"I do a lot of phone sales. I have to put in the effort, of course, for it to be blessed, for it to work. My phone sales remind me of playing the slot machine and the coins pour out of the slot machine. I just keep calling. And eventually, it works.

"I think you have to do at least three to five things a day to make anything work. I follow up and it all comes together. It eventually happens. Like a squirrel storing nuts, you do enough work and then you have enough to rely on. That's how it works for me."

Susan doesn't sell out of desperation or fear. She sells from a place of abundance and safety.

Outrageous Enthusiasm

Sales training teaches that "enthusiasm" is created with the last five letters of the actual word "siasm." Trainers say it stands for, "Yes! I am sold myself!" Until we are positive, enthusiastic, and confident in our product or service, we cannot create successful sales or negotiations.

People who are positive, upbeat, cheerfull, and optimistic are called "sales types" in this world. If you're not naturally that way, it behooves you to consider altering your personality a bit to encompass the more endearing traits of the sales professional.

Ask yourself a few questions before you leap into the negotiation:

1. Do you really want to work with this company/person?

2. If you had a choice, would you be selling/negotiating this product/service?

3. Do you believe in what you're about to say in the negotiation? Is your service the best? Is your product exemplary?

4. Do you like the people you'll be working with? Have you met them?

5. Do you trust these people? If they say it will be done on the 16th, do you believe it will be? Or do you think they will be coming up with excuses between now and then to justify failure to perform?

6. Is the deal fair?

7. If it is fair, what's the ultimate upside for you, and for your company or family?

The answers to these questions must be squarely faced. The less prevarication on your part, the less the deal will wobble. If you aren't completely sure you want this deal, if you aren't 100-percent committed to backing up your side of the deal, if you can't be completely sure it's worth the effort it will take to close and complete it, you shouldn't be negotiating.

The Power of Position

Remember when your mom turned to you and said, "Because I said so!"? Maybe that was her reason for anything, or maybe it was out of exasperation, but "because I said so" works effectively on little kids because they know Mom controls the situation.

And then the understanding of this control goes underground. Men refer to this as "pecking order" which sounds like it has more to do with poultry than negotiations. Men tend to be socialized to accept that the biggest, richest, tallest, smartest, fastest, whatever-est man automatically controls the relevant situation. Think about all the times you've seen movies or real life where the younger man is subservient to the "big boss."

Women don't socialize this way. We see someone with perkier breasts and we wonder where she bought them. We see a woman who is richer and we wonder who she married. We see a woman who runs marathons and we wonder if she maybe neglects her toddler and her husband. We tend to undermine one another, not elevate. That's unfortunate, and something we all need to eradicate, but the natural "pecking order" is not as clear with women as it is with men.

This is too bad from a woman-to-woman harmony point of view, but it also slows us down in negotiations. We neither automatically respect the other woman's position, nor consider it or consider our own.

When you are pulled over by a female police officer and you've been speeding, who has more power? She does.

When you go to small claims court over a contractor's bad work and the female judge decides the contractor was wrong, who has the power? She does.

When your elementary school teacher sent you to the principal's office, who had the power? She did.

But why do the officer, the judge, and the teacher have power? Because we agree she does. The society around us agrees she does. Are there people who try to outrun the officer, don't obey the judge, or become truant students? Of course. But most people have the authority they have because *other people gave it to them.*

The officer had to go through training to get her badge. The badge gives her authority over you and all the other drivers, including 250-pound hairy truck drivers from Oklahoma who could kill her with one bare hand.

If power is by consent, it's a secret tool, a message for you, a technique you can use to have power in many of your negotiations: **You have the power.** You have it because other people gave it to you, and it's now yours to wield. You have the power because you accepted it.

The big event is realizing who has leverage. In a buying situation, whether it's a car, a washing machine, or a yacht, you have the power. Why? Because you have the money, the credit rating, whatever it is. Therefore, you are the most powerful person in the negotiation. If you walk, everyone suffers. You've heard the motto "the customer is always right." Guess what? You are! And if you are patronizing a business that doesn't agree, leave.

Remember whose side you're on and which side of the desk you're on! You have the authority, just like the officer, the judge, and the teacher.

When negotiating with your spouse, you have power you can choose to use or not use. Among other powers, you have the power of the household. You are the determinant whether or not the relationship is harmonious, the household runs smoothly, and things that are your job get done.

When negotiating with your boss, you are also in power. This is because you have performed your role well. Good employees are very hard to find. If you do poor work, you have no leverage.

As you enter any negotiation, ask yourself precisely how much power you have. A realistic analysis may show that you have far more power than you realize. The French have a saying about this that sums up power in all sorts of relationships and situations, and is apt to this discussion:

> There is always one who kisses,
> and one who offers the cheek.
> —French Proverb

The more cheek-offering you're doing, the less kissing (up) you will have to do.

Her Majesty Will See You Now

One of the most consistent problems with women in negotiation is that we often fail to be "big enough." We forget that the reason we got the audience by using our "better" is because we are "better" than we think we are.

Reading a shelf or two of self-help books for women, one could surmise that most of us suffer from low self-esteem. Even if we've learned to hide it, it slips out around the edges like a skirt lining busting loose.

You need to put on airs if you aren't succeeding in most of your negotiations. Do not be haughty, for that will get you nowhere, but be regal, especially with men who are older than you. That will certainly get you out of the "little girl" role and into the "Yes, Ma'am!" role.

> "Boys' games teach them to develop their physical power; girls' games don't. Thus men are more apt to comfortably stride into the room, sit down and look large."
> —Gale Evans,
> *Play Like a Man, Win Like A Woman*

Our posture says a lot about our feelings about ourselves. Anyone who has been to an Anthony Robbins seminar knows that countless times, the audience is asked to leap out of their seats, break into cheering, and to stand as if they felt totally confident, totally in control. People start screaming and shouting. It's like a huge revival meeting in the old South!

But the principle behind this fervor is a sound one often cited by many motivational gurus:

> We must act ourselves
> into a better way of feeling.

Tony also teaches us that to change our mood, we need to change our bodies. He says, "Emotion is created by motion." If you walk into a negotiation looking scared, feeling small, and wondering if there is lipstick on your teeth or if you turned off the coffee pot, guess what? The other party can smell your fear, your insecurity.

You thought only bears, wild dogs, and jaguars could do it? Wrong!

You walk in looking, feeling, acting scared, you will lose!

You must prepare to walk into your negotiation situation 100-percent confident, 100-percent assured, and 100-percent regal. The bigger the stakes, the more regal you need to be.

If you want to succeed in negotiations, you will simply need to learn to turn on the majesty of your own being—at least on occasion. Of course, you may decide you like it so well that you do it all the time, and change your whole life in the process!

Power of Posture

When I was a gawky 16-year-old, my wise mother sent me to a six-week modeling course. I learned how to eat soup, apply eye shadow, and sit like a lady. The most important thing was how to walk like a runway model. Runway models might look like they need to eat more often, but they sure don't look like they are lacking in confidence. Learn the tricks they've learned to transform your business results. Walking like a queen is the easiest and handiest business skill I've ever used.

When I have to walk into a room where I'm scared or nervous, I immediately revert to this old training. Phyllis Davis, former model and author of *E2: Using the Power of Ethics And Etiquette in American Business* (Entrepreneur Press, 2002), gets into specifics, but the abridged version is:

Imagine your head, vertebrae, and pelvis are all brightly colored big wooden blocks (the kind kids play with).

Imagine your spinal cord is a rope and that a giant has strung you from pelvis to the crown of your head, like a marionette.

When the giants lifts you off the ground, all the blocks align, shoulders naturally back, tummy tucked in. You breathe deeper. You stand taller. Your posture is admirable by anyone's standards. You look like you own the whole world.

Now walk from your hips, not your knees.

Watch out, Ms. Universe! Practice a few times with a book on your head, just like in the black and white movies. Walk around with the latest Grisham novel on your head until you can align your spine and walk smoothly with it up there. When you walk into a meeting, a presentation, a sales pitch, a blind date, or anywhere you are feeling nervous, walk in like a queen.

When you walk into a meeting, be as tall as you can be, all blocks aligned. Sit down as if you were the queen herself, and gently cross your ankles and tuck them under your chair a few inches, maintaining a straight back and upright head. The first 30 seconds make all the impression, which is not to invite you to slouch afterward, but you can relax a bit after you've wowed your humble subjects. It works on women and on men. When I want them to, people often tell me they've never seen such impressive posture as mine. I don't usually admit it's a trick I use when I am tired or nervous.

You may think it's silly, but next time you walk into any public place, practice and notice if people don't turn to you with a smile of admiration and respect. Then, when you're confident, it will work when you go into a negotiation, too!

Now, let's consider a woman's "trick of the trade."

> "You cannot dominate Fortune, but you must act as if your own actions are going to be decisive."
> —Michael Ledeen,
> *Machiavelli on Modern Leadership*

Act As If

Before a man walks into a meeting, he gives himself a little pep talk about how he's going to close the negotiation, win the sale, make the deal. It's conditioning he may have acquired when being coached in high school basketball or football.

Maybe you weren't an athlete in school. Maybe you haven't learned yet that every game is mental, there is nothing else. In his life-changing classic, *Think and Grow Rich*, Napoleon Hill teaches us that our "thoughts create our reality."

If you think you're beaten, you are. If you think you'll win, you will.

You've heard the term getting "psyched." You may have spent time on the sidelines as a cheerleader—as I did—helping psyche someone else up to win. It's time to become your own cheerleading squad!

Before every speech I give, I always do something similar to this, so that the audience hears and benefits from the message and the right words fall on fallow soil. In advance of every book I put up for sale, or the start of every book negotiation, I do the same.

Before you go into a negotiating event (and this will work any time you have a lot at stake on any meeting, presentation, or the like) plan a few moments to psych yourself up. That means, you are organized enough to get to wherever you need to be early. Remember:

On time is late for leaders.
—Unknown

You're there early. You're prepared. You're dressed appropriately. Your hair and nails are looking good. You feel professional from head to toe. You...go into the ladies room.

Yep. That's where I do my praying/psyching myself up/self-talk—whatever you want to call it.

Go into the ladies room and find yourself an empty stall. Sit down, shut your eyes, and do this in precisely this sequence:

1. Visualize yourself walking into the negotiation location tall, confident, like a beauty queen with an encyclopedia on her head. You're looking like you own the whole darn world, because you do.

2. You sit down, poised. Secretly, the others are admiring your charisma and grace. You are not a woman with whom to be trifled.

3. Imagine yourself saying the perfect words at the perfect time. You may want to rehearse a prepared phrase or two, or you can just visualize using perfect words.

4. Now imagine the other parties smiling. Nodding their heads. Laughing at your wit. Imagine them yanking out a pen and signing that check, contract, or whatever is at stake.

Take a deep breath. Imagine you have an invisible perfume atomizer. It's made from lovely crystal, perfectly etched. As you exhale, imagine the power and energy of this happiness you now feel is being drawn into the atomizer. Feel its long silk purple cord with a tassel expand in your hand as the positive essence of your success is inhaled into the atomizer.

Open your eyes. You have captured your power in this crystal bottle.

Now, feet flat on the floor, shut your eyes again. Pray, meditate, wish, dream, imagine the following words:

> *It is my dominant desire that every person involved in and affected by this negotiation have their needs met at the highest possible level. I see this transaction working out in its own perfect time, for the highest good of all concerned. So be it.*

Stand up, go to the mirror, and check your teeth for lipstick and your lips for a million dollar smile. Check your clothes to make sure you look as you want to look. Lift your imaginary atomizer, give yourself a spritz, and go knock 'em dead!

In Summary

Your attitude is absolutely critical in predicting the success of your negotiations. This means taking time to prepare your facts, your case, your self, your words, and the event itself as much as possible.

CHAPTER 13

Here's Lookin' at You

"You walked in the room and right then I knew, I
finally found somebody for me. But to tell you the
truth, I didn't know what to do. Should I turn
around or should I leave?"
—Rod Stewart's "You're in My Heart"

We're driving to school at 7:40 a.m. on a Tuesday. My 11-year-old daughter tells me she *knows* it's going to be a good day at school today. I ask her why. She looks at me like I've missed a page in the script and says, "Mom! Because I'm wearing my new skirt!"

So she goes on to have a good day.

Last time you bought a new outfit—one in your own size, not two sizes too small—how did it feel to wear it? College kids just graduating are told to buy an "interview" suit. It impresses the future employer and makes them feel more confident when they come for the interview.

When I was about to appear on CBS's *The Early Show*, one of many TV shows I've had the honor of being a guest on, I noticed something important. No matter how you look when you walk in, the makeup room people always tell you that you look terrific. Their positive banter continues, a joke here, a touch of blush there. They are fixing you up to look your very best to play the role that you are about to play.

I didn't notice it until that day at CBS, but in retrospect, the makeup artists *at Politically Incorrect*, FOX, *Crosstalk*—pretty much everywhere—all said roughly the same thing to me, making me feel good about myself before I went on live national television.

When you're going after the big fish in a negotiation, don't you deserve the same treatment? People notice chipped nails, stringy frizzy hair, badly done makeup, cheaply made clothes, colors that clash with skin tone, and smears of foundation down a woman's neck. They notice details, and the longer you sit with them, the more details they have time to notice.

Women are most likely to judge you as sloppy, lazy, or disorganized if you aren't looking impeccable at an important negotiation. If you walk into the car dealership or the client's office looking like part of the janitorial staff, chances are you'll be treated like you are. If you walk in looking like you've just lunched with Ivana Trump, chances are you'll be treated that way, too. Think about Julia Roberts before her transformation in *Pretty Woman*. Remember her shopping nightmare on Rodeo Drive?

Men may not notice the tiny details, and we all have known men who wouldn't notice if we dyed our hair purple, but even they pick up the "essence" of a woman's style. You have to decide on clothes, hair, makeup, nails, and you have to be in top form.

There's no better investment in the success of your career than to look professional every day. There's no easier way to ensure you are treated like a professional than to look like one. If you want to be taken seriously, look like a serious player.

Some good examples of serious players to consider would be attorney Gloria Allred, known political figures, news anchors, and other women often in the public eye. Bad examples would be Courtney Love, Mary Ann on Gilligan's Island, any Goth teenager, and your average rap music diva.

You can balk at the concept of a uniform, of looking like an elegant version of everyone else. But eventually, you'll realize that the women who are making the money *look* like the women who are making the money.

Seeing is believing. Hire an image consultant if you don't know what to do, or have an elegant (not necessarily fashionable) friend take you shopping and advise you. It may be the single most effective decision you ever make about how you present yourself to the world.

Image is perception
and perception is everything!

Here's a simple example. By now, you've probably heard of La Perla lingerie. A single pair of La Perla thong panties—with less than 2 inches of lace or silk in the whole garment—can cost you upwards of $100 per pair.

You can get a six-pack of good old 100-percent cotton panties at Target for $8.

Both, essentially, perform the same function.

If you're a Target kind of girl, you could happily wear the less expensive panties, thinking of the $92 you saved. If you're a La Perla kind of girl, you could swear their panties make you sexier, thinner, prettier, and more toned.

Which is true? Whichever you believe is true!

One pair is not better than the other. But how many times do you see a well-dressed, well-groomed woman wearing a well-fitted, exquisitely cut suit and say, "Wow! She's impressive!" Probably every single time.

On the other side, you probably never see a woman traipsing along in gym shoes, baggy pink sweat pants, and an old blue sweatshirt and think, "Wow! She's impressive."

What you wear, how you walk, how you move, how you smile, the dignity of your carriage, the cut and style of your hair, are all things that affect how the world sees you, and thus how you are treated. We are treated by others as well as we require them to treat us.

Buy one fabulous suit, in the size you wear, not the size you hope to wear after losing 10 more pounds. Regularly get your hair done by professionals who have a high level of skill. Get one pair of the most expensive famous label shoes you can afford. Buy the perfectly matching handbag. Make sure your nails are perfectly neat. You may not wear 3-inch acrylic nails with kitties airbrushed on them, unless most of the women in your industry have those nails! Look the part. It's a role you're playing, like Nicole Kidman or Charlize Theron. You are your own costuming department.

Go to the Web and look up pictures of Gloria Allred or Geraldine Ferraro or Condaleeza Rice or other women of highest distinction in our culture. You want to be a winner? Dress like the winners. You'll feel better, look better, and exude confidence.

There's no difference between your brain and a better-dressed woman's brain. She may conduct herself with more panache than you did up until now, and the world steps aside to accommodate her. Join in!

The Power of Pink

When I was 12 years old, my mother's dearest friend was a little old lady in her early 80s. Mrs. Nina Angel (her real name!) lived just a few miles from our house in Prescott, Ariz., in a pale yellow clapboard house with a few red plastic geraniums out front. She had soft, wispy white hair, which she wore in a bun, and skin that looked like crumpled crepe paper. She wore old-fashioned clothes and drove a white car as big as a tank. Mrs. Angel had one of those huge sofas she called a "davenport," covered with hard little nubs of fabric flecked with gold string. Along its sturdy back it wore lacy white antimacassars she had crocheted herself. It was as uncomfortable to sit on in summer shorts as it was to look at.

I can't remember where she was from, but I do remember her manner of speaking, sort of lilting and then staccato, interchanged. She'd seem docile and old-ladylike, and then you'd see a flash of her very bright side. "Sharp as a tack," she would have said. One day, I obediently sat on her painful davenport sipping weak, bitter lemonade and listened to my mother and Mrs. Angel talk.

My mother was concerned that Mrs. Angel's car was not working properly. Mom was busily promising my dad's services to "come take a look at it" right away, and suggested she shouldn't drive in the meantime.

Mrs. Angel laughed and said, "Why, don't you know, Carol? I have a secret weapon!" She got up sprightly, opened a closet near the front door, and yanked out a pink sweater. She held it forward and laughed triumphantly. To our blank stares at the garment, she smiled and said, "Men can't resist stopping to help a woman wearing pink. I always have something pink with me when I'm out driving. It works every time!"

We laughed, but Mrs. Angel's little "trick" has proven itself repeatedly in my life. And I'd like to add, they can scarcely not stop to help to carry luggage for a woman in heels and an above-the-knee skirt. (I believe this single truth is responsible for more women dressing nicely when traveling solo than any other.)

Mrs. Angel in her quaint, old-fashioned way brought to light an important principle in negotiation. Perhaps one of the biggest advantages to being a woman in a negotiation with men is the very fact that we are women. Over and over, women told me that they "play like the boys" to earn respect in a negotiation, or conversely that they "pull out the femininity" and suddenly do the damsel in distress routine. That is, they put on the pink sweater.

It is our very ability to be versatile that can set the negotiation just a little off guard, make the fellow we're dealing with a little unsure of his stance. My daughter already knows this organically when she flutters her eyelashes at a male neighbor asking him to stop what he's doing and come help her fix her bookshelf.

Women have an extraordinary power to move quickly across the spectrum from ultra-feminine to as tough as any guy. A man doing the same would seem a lunatic, or worse. A woman doing this simply stuns the prey, like a cobra mesmerizing its victim-to-be.

"On his affair with a local woman, Machiavelli wrote, 'Everything seems easy to me, and to her every desire, no matter how different to that which should be mine, I conform. And though I seem to have entered great trouble, I feel in it such sweetness.'"
—Michael Ledeen,
Machiavelli on Modern Leadership

When we enter a negotiation, we can intuitively assess the situation. We can consider whether our own needs would be best served by applying more of the gentle, feminine side of ourselves, or by accessing the stronger, more masculine side. Negotiation is a case in which opposites certainly do attract a better deal. Learning to leverage our strength as females, and the variety of approaches open to us, gives us additional power.

When we negotiate with other women, the situation changes a bit. Women of course are aware of the range of which we are capable, and bring different issues to the negotiation. The point of a negotiation is to get what you came for, and give what you can reasonably allow to go. Remembering this is the Holy Grail of negotiation will certainly keep you from blustering about the core principles of the feminist movement when it is suggested you use your feminine wiles when they are helpful. When it comes to negotiation, if you've got it, honey, flaunt it…to a point.

People didn't stop to help Mrs. Angel because she was sexy, or because they thought they might get anything more than a home-made cookie and a sweet smile as a thank you. She was simply using a time-tested feminine ability to appeal to a man's sense of dignity and pride. Who's to say that's not why we have the skill in the first place?

Your goal is to use your feminine powers to get the other side on your side.

In his powerful, eye-opening book, *Why Customers Come Back*, (Career Press, 2004) Manzie Lawfer explains the how and why of the truth that "people buy from people they like." Our job is to make it easy for the other party to like us, to want to help us. This means using all the resources at our disposal, including pink sweaters!

Pretty in Pantsuits, too!

Former National Association of Women Business Owners President Bonnie Paul, who is also a very successful entrepreneur, agreed to be interviewed for this book. In that delightful hour she told me she believes, "It's a double-edged sword being female. It can be difficult being taken seriously sometimes when you are better looking than average. I have to be very careful when I am negotiating with men that I read them correctly and exhibit a demeanor that is showing that

I am self-assured and I know what I am doing, but I am not a ball buster. There is a softness that has to come across, wrapped in self-assuredness.

"I prefer to negotiate with men instead of women. With women, I have to gauge their situation relevant to me. I have to be sure not to threaten them with my self or my clothes. You have to downplay any attractiveness because you could get removed from consideration if there is a jealousy factor in there.

"You have to be smart in how you approach the person with whom you are working. With a woman, you want to bring forward the professionalism that will make her look good to her bosses, because you are going to help her achieve what she wants to achieve. Be dead on and straight on and very self assured.

"I dress based on the audience. I make sure I wear something that is very professional suit-wise. I make sure that it is appropriate. I guess I would allow a softness to come through a bit more if I was seeing a man instead of a woman. I generally prefer pantsuits.

"In terms of jewelry or not, I try to hit the middle ground—not too flashy, not too plain. I know that my overall demeanor comes across, because I have studied it. I've used others as a mirror. I come across as a class act. I try to dress down a little bit so I am not intimidating. Because I am confident, I can be intimidating. So I try to dress nicely without labels or identifiable clothes.

"When I headed the National Association of Women Business Owners, there was some concern with our corporate partners that when I represent NAWBO that I might not dress the part.

"They were conservative, and they had seen me be a little bit more flamboyant. Each business and industry has its own style. I know my audience. I know how to dress for X instead of Y. There's this whole banker side vs. artsy side. You've got to study your audience. You've got to know who is on the other side of the desk.

"Dress conservatively and use the first few minutes to know how your demeanor should come across for the rest of the interview.

"I immediately size up who I'm seeing. If I can't get info in advance, I use the first few moments of chit-chat to structure the rest of my presentation. You let them lead off the conversation and you match their personality, and their approach to doing business."

What size is your audience?

How we come across as women can range from "ball buster" to "pink sweater," and there's a need to be able to play both ranges and everything in the middle. It's the difference between a film starring Mel Gibson and a Merchant Ivory production.

If you are more of a girly-girl type, and already own lots of pink, and know how to giggle, you probably have trouble being taken seriously. You might be passed over for promotions. You perhaps have wondered why less qualified women than you move faster up the chain, or seem to get more of what they want in life.

If you are more masculine in your approach to life, if you are seen as "no fun" and "all serious" and you tend to wear lots of gray and black suits, have short hair, and use a no-nonsense approach, perhaps you are also not well-liked because your severity alarms people. "All work and no play make Jill a dull girl." The truth of the statement, "People do business with people they like" cannot be overemphasized.

Something as simple as changing the balance between the feminine and masculine in your clothing and personal style can make a world of difference in the results you are getting.

If your current persona at work or in negotiations isn't getting you what you want, it's time for a change. Remember this life-changing rule:

> If your current actions were enough to produce
> more of what you want, more of it would
> already be in your life.
> —Unknown

The Power of Your Voice

My dear, precious friend Jana Collins, one of the most sincere, honest, and hard-working book publicists in the free world, has a voice that makes her sound like she's 14 years old. Jana's a grown woman, with a child of her own and a large staff. She jokes about her "little girl" voice and how people never believe she is who she is until they meet her.

I recently introduced Jana to another friend, Patricia, who is a soft-spoken, blonde-haired, blue-eyed, sweethearted woman. She's written a book, the profits of which go to encourage literacy among children. At the executive women's luncheon at which I met her I was impressed before she spoke with how kind and gentle she looked. Even her clothes and hairstyle spoke "girlish" to me.

When Patricia introduced herself, I discovered she has a sweet little girl voice, too. No one could ever take that voice seriously. But when she told me who she is and what she has accomplished in her life, I was struck by the wisdom, maturity, and philanthropy of her vision. Her Hollywood credentials are impressive, and it's not easy to be impressed in my town. Then she told me she's also been asked to be the "Storytelling Princess" for a children's program. This woman's IQ is probably off the charts! How wrong anyone would be to judge her by appearances or magic wands as being as coy as one might think.

She and Jana hit it off at once, and shared laughter about their "little girl voices." Here are two competent professional women who recognize the liability their soft voices are in the business world.

The less there is for the other party to have to overcome, the easier it is for them to transact business with you. If you are blessed with a "Fairy Princess" voice, you are welcome to use it for story hour at the library, and for cooing at your own little ones. But if you feel it is distracting to people, especially men with whom you are trying to do business, you may wish to try some techniques.

Steven Memel is a voice coach to the stars and a friend of mine. Some of the techniques below are his and some I learned when hanging around other voice coaches:

1. Practice saying hello at deeper, deeper, deeper notes, then higher, higher, higher notes. You may wish to use a piano to help you. This shows you the range you can use. Practice a few times.

2. As if you were meditating, take a deep breath in, hold it for a count of three, and let it out while making the sound "Oh" until you are out of breath. Repeat this four or five times, until it tickles your lungs and you can feel it reverberating inside you. This is the depth of your voice.

3. Pick a male singer and practice singing along with him. Don't worry, you won't grow a mustache. By trying to match his range, you will learn more about your voice and its ability to move. (Prince, Michael Jackson, John Denver, and Paul Simon are not good for this exercise. Pavarotti, Billy Joel, Don Henley and George Strait will work fine.)

4. Think back to those times when your mother used your whole name in that specific tone of voice she used when you were in trouble. "Wendy Louise Keller!" meant I was in for it—big time. Maybe you use it with your children, but "that tone" has power, authority, and strength. Use it for fun and profit.

5. Take a deep breath, hold it for 7 counts, and let it out for 14 counts. Repeat this 10 times. Then try any of the above again.

Breathing plays a big part in vocal range. Air going through your voice box creates the sound other people hear. You already know your voice sounds far different to all of us than it does to you. No one says you *have* to deepen your voice to be credible, but if you have the ability to do it when you want to make a point (with your kids, your spouse, or your negotiation partner) it's a nice skill to have.

> "If you have to, go and talk to a blank wall...Speak loudly enough so that if there were someone in the room, no matter where he or she was, you could be heard. Throughout corporate America, women speak from the place called no-permission. We speak softly, we speak timidly, without authority or power."
> —Gail Evans,
> *Play Like a Man, Win Like a Woman*

Feel, Felt, Found

Bonnie Paul, whom you may recall provides high end art to commercial and private collectors, said, "One year I was negotiating with a company to acquire their art. My competitor was also bidding to do the same. In the end, they chose her. I found out a while later it was because her hourly rate was lower.

"I thought about that for a while. The next year, they were planning to choose her again. I called the decision-maker. I said, "If the only difference between us is the hourly price, how do you know that I am not twice as fast? That I am not three times more efficient? That I don't have better contacts? Time can be padded. Results are what count. I got the deal."

You can use the words you choose as "power statements" that command respect and let people know you mean business.

Some experts advise women not to "show too much teeth when smiling in the first few minutes of a business meeting"; not to appear "too excited or eager to be there"; to remember to "breath at a relaxed and regulated rate"; and to "use power words to gain immediate respect." All of that is good advice.

Power statements come in lots of good shapes and sizes. Try these out in front of a mirror.

"More to the point here…"

"As I explained to Jim yesterday…"

"How well does this option solve the problem?"

"What works better for me is…"

"What I'd like to see here is…"

"If I can do that, are you ready to commit to…"

"The benefit to your company is…"

"I understand how you feel about that. Others have felt the same way. What they found works best is…"

"Now, to be absolutely certain I'm clear on your meaning, let me repeat. You said…"

"You are obviously a successful woman/skilled negotiator/wise shopper/good manager."

There's an excellent book on learning and using power phrases, called *Power Phrases!* by Meryl Runion (Power Potentials Publishing, 2002). She explains that in negotiations, sometimes we get so focused that we forget to hear what the other party needs and is trying to say. Just like when you are talking to a child, you need to acknowledge that you can hear the other person.

Imagine the cashier keeps saying, "Our return policy is that you have to bring it back within 30 days. I can't help you. It's been too long."

You will say, "What I'm hearing you say is that your return policy states that it has to be brought back in 30 days, even if it is broken. Is that what you said?"

The cashier says, "Yes. I'm sorry." At this instant, if it is in his or her power to refund your money, you have just gotten it back. "Yes" is a huge leap from the adversarial role in the first statement she made, and "I'm sorry" is a personally involved statement showing you've brought her round to your side.

You say, "Have you ever taken something back that was broken and been told something like this?"

She says, "Oh, yeah. A month ago I bought this CD player for my little sister, and it was totally defective. They wouldn't take it back. I was so mad!"

You say, "I can relate to how mad you were. I get mad, too, when something is broken, it's not my fault, and I can't get my money back. What would work best for me here is if you could simply refund my money and send this back to the manufacturer."

Chances are good you'll get your money back. If not, you can sure ask for the manager and repeat the same process. This sort of statement/question pattern works in every scenario. It's just a matter of being comfortable. Whether you have a strong voice, a gentle voice, or an average voice, what you say is every bit as important as how you say it.

David Sampson, who runs a large recreational vehicle store in Phoenix, Ariz. (*www.LittleDealer.com*), tells me in a negotiation with a customer, he uses the classic "Feel, Felt, Found" to help his customers understand the benefits of the trailer they want to buy. He says, "It helps them to feel confident about their decision." What he's really doing is building rapport, and overcoming objections the customer might have to the sale.

It goes something like this. The customer says, "I am concerned that I might not use the RV as much as I would like, and then it would be a waste of money sitting in my driveway." Applying the "Feel, Felt, Found" method, David would say, "I understand exactly how you feel. I have had many customers in the past who have felt that same way. But what they have found is that because it is so much easier to go on trips because they don't have to load up all their stuff and go through all the hassles, now they can go out more often. Now they don't have to worry about the ground being uneven or the hassle of...."

This shows the person with whom you are negotiating that you do understand his concern, that it is not unique, and that others who have had the same concerns have had better results than they even anticipated.

This rapport is what drives people to understand that you are fairminded and rational. It is also what helps you smooth out your negotiation bumps on the path to success.

In Summary

Until people know what an amazing, powerful, smart woman you are, they are going to judge the book by its cover. Make sure you look, sound, act, and move the part of the woman you are and the world will lay roses at your feet.

CHAPTER 14

Location, Location, Location

"You can't build a reputation
on what you're going to do."
—Henry Ford, (1863-1947)
Industrialist, entrepreneur

In 1995, I was hot on the trail of a big-deal CEO. His business auto-biography would bring me some major cash and a lot of recognition in my industry. I was beside myself with passion for this negotiation.

While it's true that most would-be authors want a literary agent way more than the agent wants them, in Mr. Big's case, the tables were turned. I dearly wanted to handle him, and so did a few other agents.

It came down to me and two others. Mr. Big determined this was an important decision, and he would fly to Los Angeles to meet me in my office, meet my staff, and see our operation.

I'd been divorced less than 10 months. The business had grown from 700 square feet on my property with four employees to our first big commercial lease with nine people. It had happened so fast, and there was so much turmoil in my personal life, I hadn't yet stopped to think how it might look to an outsider.

Mr. Big showed up at our office and was led into my swanky office with its view of the next door strip mall's parking lot. My office furnishings were a tapestry armchair given to me by a neighbor, a brand new luxurious mahogany desk, a rickety metal TV tray holding a dying plant, and a top-of-the-line computer. It was an odd mix, and it reflected the meteoric success we'd had so far. It was like my life as I emerged from the divorce—half old and yucky, half new and shining.

Mr. Big came in and sat down in the tapestry chair. He looked around. The pink tapestry really clashed with the industrial beige carpet. I'd never noticed.

He stood up after 10 minutes of conversation. He said, "I can't do business with someone who can work in an office like this. You look like you're barely making it."

He left. With him went my dreams for that big commission check, which had included upgrading my staff's motley collection of desks and tables into a matching set.

I learned an important lesson that day. That's one mistake I've never made again. Whether it is right or wrong, people judge others on appearances.

Almost in direct contrast, in January 2004 we moved into 1,600 square feet in what is considered the most prestigious office space in Los Angeles County. We have a view of 20 miles of Pacific Ocean beach, prime shopping and tourist area, absolutely luxurious appointments, exquisite desks, top-of-the-line computers and a whole wall of glass looking at the beach from our sixth-floor suite.

Three weeks into the new space, a man who is a hot-shot business consultant to huge companies came into my field of vision with his book and speaking ideas. I invited him over to the office for a chat.

Forty-five minutes later, he was ready to sign a contract. He said, "If you're doing this well for yourself, you must know something I don't about how the publishing and speaking industries work. I want to learn from you."

When I was just starting out, I couldn't have afforded the big fancy office at the beach. I met clients in restaurants because I was working from home, and had a baby to raise. **The sixth negotiation principle illustrated here is to show your best self.** Your choice of venue is critical. If you don't have any money, buy just one perfect outfit and invite the client to meet you for coffee at 2 or 3 p.m. (any time that is *not* meals or drinks time) at the nicest place in driving range for both of you.

Ideally, you'll want to use the venue for the negotiation to your advantage. You are at a disadvantage at their office, because they can be distracted with work on their desk, colleagues, ringing phones, emergencies, and so on.

Cindy Montgomery, who sells high quality stationery to office supply shops in Arizona, said, "I had a customer who drove me nuts. I liked her as a person, I even liked her husband. But she drove me nuts. I'd go to her shop to show her my new line, but she would accept every single interruption. She couldn't concentrate for more than five minutes. Eventually, I just stopped seeing her. Now she orders over the phone. I still get my commission, but meeting her at her place was just too much. It wasn't worth the effort and frustration."

If your place isn't ideal or you can't get them to make the drive, pick the nicest neutral territory you can. If you think it will be a lengthy negotiation and there are a number of people, rent a board room in a nice hotel close to the client. The more control you have over the venue, the easier it will be for you to feel confident and control the client's experience.

When I train professional speakers, I teach them that they are in charge of everything at the event. The lighting (bright enough so people don't get drowsy), the room temperature (68 degrees), the seating arrangements, the A/V equipment—everything. Without taking total responsibility, things that distract the event or meeting or training can cause people to have a less than optimal outcome.

I recently gave a training in a hotel. I was paying $500 for a reasonably small room for a very high-end training. My class's attention and results were critical. Halfway through the morning, the noise of a jackhammer began destroying our concentration. I went around the hotel to find the manager, who told me it was the people in the building next door. I complained that it was disturbing our concentration. She had it suspended for the rest of the day—within 15 minutes the noise had stopped.

The Honor of
Your Presence Is Requested

Respect is essential in a negotiation. Make the other party comfortable, but not too comfortable. If you want to add some nice touches, depending on the nature of the negotiation (try flowers, colored table cloths), make it a pleasant environment.

Gerard I. Nierenberg, in his classic book *The Complete Negotiator,* says, "Your regard for the opposer is evidenced by what happens after you first invite her or him to a meeting in your home territory. Have you assisted in travel plans? Booked reservations? The climate of settlement is established even before the meeting opens."

What is the difference between the best French restaurant in your town and a fast food place? At the fast food place, you know you'll get plastic, bright colors, and mediocre cheap food. But it's still food, and you take your kids there. At the French restaurant, you will get ambient lighting, good service, excellent food and wine, a white table cloth, and none of your food will be wrapped in paper. You'll take your lover there.

The facility you choose or agree to negotiate in should be comfortable for everyone concerned. Neither party wants to feel they are in "hostile territory" about to be ambushed. Personally, there's no harm in making it a little nicer than what you figure the client expects. It gives you a subtle upper hand.

What if You're Going *There*?

What if the situation requires you to meet them on their territory? Traveling salespeople, for instance, have to walk into a strange environment, get comfortable immediately, and transmit that relaxation and fun energy to the people to whom they are hoping to sell.

How do they do it?

A neighbor of mine, Carrie Lincoln, sells medical supplies such as heart valves and other important apparatus. She not only has to go to the doctors' offices, but often finds herself actually in the surgery room helping the doctor understand how to correctly use the apparatus!

That's got to be tough!

I interviewed Carrie. She is a very attractive tall woman, with blonde hair. "The first trick is to be prepared," Carrie says. "Know your stuff. Know your material, your product, your goal up one side and down the other. I know that the product we sell is the best there is, and I can explain why. I do it without any sort of fanfare, but I show them a big stack of research that proves it's the best.

"Walking into a new doctor's office is sort of a strange experience. You don't know what you'll find. Because I have to overcome them hitting on me and get straight to business right away, I don't ever smile with an open mouth. I also never 'ease up' or 'chill out.' Everything is completely business-like. They know I'm not there to play. I'm there to work. One doctor recently wrote my boss and said he was impressed with me. That made me feel really good."

Confidence in your product, in your person, and in your posture are important factors. But what if you walk into a place that's far different than what you expected? Let's say there are piles of paper, books, and a mess everywhere you look. There's no place to sit down and the person you're there to see motions that you should sit in a chair covered with stacks of things.

Of course you will sit down, calmly moving the items off the chair while you keep up a conversation of pleasantries. If the party apologizes for the mess, you can acknowledge it by saying, "Oh, you should see my office sometime!" or if that's too far from true, you could make a joke and say, "It's just so hard to find good cleaning help these days, isn't it?"

If the other person offers you coffee, tea, water, or a Danish pastry that's been sitting out since the Nixon era, your line is, "Yes, thank you." Women make a mistake of not accepting things that are offered to us. Sometimes, it's because we don't want the person offering it to us—someone's secretary usually—to feel like we think she's "beneath" us or that she's our servant. Or we don't want someone to go to the trouble. Men don't do this. Men always say, "Yes, thanks. I'll take it black." They may take two sips or half a bite the entire time, but they do it. Especially if the other person is eating or drinking, too. It's an unwritten rule.

Being smart, you will have arrived early so the meeting doesn't begin with everyone waiting for you to get out of the ladies room. You will also match your breathing rate to the rate of the most important person in the room. (More on this in Chapter 15.) You will put the things you are carrying on the table or on the floor, sit calmly, and survey the room in a relaxed manner.

You have now created an aura of relaxed, poised confidence in yourself. No one wants you to come in, sit on the edge of your seat, litter their desk at once with your literature and statistics, and show your enthusiasm by boring your eyes into their skull. The more "at home" you look, the more at home the other person will feel in their own habitat.

In Summary

The best place to have a negotiation is in a place of your choice—your office. If that's not possible, the next best choice is a neutral territory. The final choice is the other party's office or place of business. Your power decreases with each step. You can overcome this disadvantage by appearing poised and completely at ease.

CHAPTER 15

Creating Instant Rapport

> "There's an assumption that 'negotiation' means 'battle,' or that it's got to be 'intense' or 'tense.' I always like to use humor. There's something funny about everything. At the most tense moments, I like to bring everyone back and let their humanness catch up."
>
> —Jeanne Coughlin,
> *The Rise of Women Entrepreneurs*

Dr. Debbie Ciavola is a well-regarded family therapist in Dallas, Tex. She's also the author of the book, *Connecting with Your Teen* (New Harbinger, 2002). Her job is a tough one. People who come to see her are in the midst of tough family problems. They are talking about divorce, or real problems with their child. Creating a comfortable emotional environment is crucial, and the faster the better. This is important for you to learn when you walk into a negotiation situation yourself.

Dr. Ciavola and I met for an interview for this book. She says, "People come in to see me, and I've never met them before. They are coming in because something is going wrong in their life. I have to join with people immediately so they feel comfortable talking to me. I'm also a divorce mediator. There are a lot of things people can do to facilitate the whole process and keep the emotion out of it.

"I watch the other person's body language. In 20 seconds we compute the rapidity of people's voice/image with characteristics of everyone similar who has gone before. We assume the person in front of us is like someone else. Watch the other person's body language because it gives you something else to focus on. Watch the seating arrangements. Think outside yourself, as an observer, not a participant. There are ways they "gesture," their feelings. There are some people who are harder to read than others. Make it easier for the other person to relate to you. The more you focus on matching their alignment, their facial expression, you are already becoming an obeserver. Don't focus on what you are feeling instead focus on what's going on with the other person.

"What ends up happening is we pay attention to what happened in the past or will happen future. When you step back, you are focusing on the now. Then you are able to stay more in control. It's the control issue people have difficulty with.

"When someone is telling me something very sad, I watch their gestures, watch their feelings. This makes my feelings diminish. A simple gesture (expose the wrist, rotate the thumb facing up), is a sign of alignment and relaxation. It helps others to feel relaxed and open. I teach my clients to use this in job interviews, etc. Who are you under stress? A talker, a pusher? Who is the other person under stress?

"If you pay attention to where they are nonverbally, you'll find that you will start aligning your body language to them, you will get more agreement than you ever believed possible.

"I try to help the other person feel comfortable. Even when you are talking about seating arrangements, some people want a desk between them. Some people want nothing but air. If someone immediately opens the space, then I open the space. If you talk to someone who is pushy and assertive, quick to close, those people are pushing for results. An analytical person will be calmer, so there's a desk between you. Your language even has to change. Watch the person's posture. If he or she is leaning forward, you won't lean forward because that seems like a challenge. Once you get into challenge mode, it will be a tough one. The goal is to match or complement his or her style. That builds connection.

"The only people you don't mirror are those who are confrontational. Start by being open to anything in the negotiation. Do this to find middle ground. If you can't get middle ground you have already withdrawn anyway and it's a waste of time. If people feel like they are aligned with you, it's amazing what they will do. Most people don't develop the people skills. When someone trips their wire, they are tripping into their past.

"If you or they close off, it stops being win-win. It's about being in the now and being fully present. You have to make immediate alignment to make something work. Most people aren't sure why someone makes them feel uncomfortable. They don't think, they just react.

"We make assumptions because of how the person looks based on how we dealt with someone like that before and had X experience.

"The past is scary and the future is uncertain, so the best we can do is stay in the now," says Dr. Ciavola. "Staying in the now helps people deal with rejection, because it isn't about *you*, it is about them. You need to come from a place of confidence, take the best you with you. Don't be concerned that you walk in with the one down position, you won't sell. They can smell it on you. It's fear.

"'Do you think it will make a difference that I walk into this job interview without a job?' a woman asked me.

"'Yes, to one person. You. Because you will walk in feeling one down.' I said.

"I've had three clients lose jobs just by negotiating via e-mail. It would be interesting to see how people would have done face-to-face. Rapport is all about creating the middle ground, finding something in common. You have to have them fall in love with you enough to make the deal. People work with people they like.

"People will give just a little bit if they feel they like you. This is why establishing rapport and maintaining it is critical. I see so many people each week in my private practice. I can't think of a time when I didn't get along with someone. I get them to do what I want them to do for themselves because I am looking for the good in the person and I've created enough rapport, so they trust me."

Julie Morgan is an account executive for a healthcare services company. When I struck up a conversation with her about negotiation and Dr. Ciavola's take on being likable, and liking others, she said, "I completely agree! If I just hard-line and make it tough for the other person to like me or to want to get a better rate from me, I will probably lose the whole deal. People want to do business with people they like. I have four rules I keep in mind when I meet a client:

1. See what's important to him.
2. Remove my own past and future.
3. Create rapport.
4. Get him to work with me."

Julie said, "I bought a car about two months ago. I realized that if my goal is just to get a specific car, I'm going to negotiate focused only on a good deal. It's going to be obvious to the salesperson. But if he thinks I'm also on his side, he's going to believe that my interest in getting a good deal involves both parties, instead of just forcing him to give me more than what he can. Everything we do isn't always about just what we need to accomplish. Animosity happens when you over-push."

Connecting With People

Creating rapport is a critical skill whether they come to you or you go to them. Lisa Johnson is a saleswoman. When she wasn't being paid on time by one of the companies whose products she sells, she had to call the company and find out what was wrong.

She said, "I try to connect with people first. I recently took up a great new line and commissions weren't paid monthly as they were promised. I spoke with the payment person and I explained my problem. Then, so she'd really get it and see what was happening to me, I asked what she would do if she'd been told she'd be paid weekly for her job, but then she got paid monthly instead. Instead of her being defensive, she was able to understand my position. She said, 'Because you haven't been awful about this, I'm going to personally see that you get a check sooner.' I always find out something I have in common with someone to ensure that they listen to me more."

Common ground is not all that difficult to find. If you're one of those people who doesn't like small talk, there are plenty of ways to find something of mutual interest to talk about with a person. Here are some very basic tips. For great ideas, I recommend you read any of the brilliant networking books mentioned in this book's bibliography.

If you are meeting the person live, comment positively and briefly on...

- ♣ Their office décor.
- ♣ The family photo on the desk.
- ♣ The door that squeaked very loudly when you walked in.
- ♣ A great piece of art on the wall.
- ♣ A funny poster or quote.
- ♣ Something that reminds you of one your mom/grandpa/ etc. used to have "just like it"—a grandfather clock, a certain type of armchair.
- ♣ A book you've read that is also on their shelf.
- ♣ A great necktie or elegant dress.
- ♣ An office plant—you can say you love plants, or you always kill them, or how did you get this one to look so robust, or, "I always think of getting a dieffenbachia for my office. How does yours do here?"
- ♣ Any non-business, not-too-personal comment on any inanimate object in the room.

Of course, being on the phone gives you a different set of "rapport cues." The *single most important* "trick" I've ever learned for creating rapport over the telephone is this: Keep a mirror on your desk for three months. Every time you pick up the phone, smile in the mirror. A big, sincere smile. Remember: It comes through in your voice! Then try the following powerful tips.

1. Introduce Yourself

The person on the other end of the phone just said, "You've reached the company. I'm Karen. How can I help you?" Even though you will shortly have to give your full name, address, and blood type, introduce yourself as you would to a new friend.

2. Use Pleasant Phrases

- ♣ "Wow, I just love your accent! Where are you from originally?"

- ♣ "What a cheerful voice! I've been in the phone queue for 20 minutes, so I know you're busy, but I can't believe you maintain such a cheerful attitude. How do you do it?"

- ♣ "You sure sound professional! I'm glad I got through to you!"

- ♣ "You know, I had to press 14 different buttons to get to you, and listen to some of the worst country western music I've ever heard. But just from the sound of your voice, I know it's going to be worth it. Thanks for being so professional."

- ♣ "Boy, if I'd known I was going to get sent to the Customer Service Supervisor and you were so nice and efficient, I'd have broken my water heater a month ago on purpose. I can't believe the great service you're giving me! Thanks!"

Think these things sound "canned" and "obvious"? Try them next time and prove me wrong. Most people who call customer service departments are *furious* and want the world to know. I worked in customer service for a newspaper when I was young, and on rainy days, hundreds of customers would call furious that their papers had gotten wet because water leaked into the bag. They'd be yelling at me—over a 25 cent newspaper! I'd never even been to their house, and it was just poor teenagers and immigrants who delivered them. They had no real reason to yell, except it apparently made them feel better. Of course we were going to send them a dry one, whether they yelled or not. So why yell?

I find in my mostly telephone sales job as a literary agent, it's always easier to make the person laugh. Laughter builds rapport, laughter allows more oxygen to the brain, and laughter creates instant friendships. Maybe that's what helped me today....

Last night I had a dinner party. I probably shouldn't have, because I knew the deadline for this book was looming. Honestly, I thought I'd be done with it and the party would be a sort of quiet celebration for completing it. After dinner, I went to wash the dishes and discovered I had no hot water! Two of the remaining guests grabbed flashlights and went with me to look at the hot water heater. Empty! Uh-oh.

I went to the kitchen to contemplate my next action. Suddenly, I heard the sound of rushing water. Lots of water. Under my house! I ran outside and sure enough, my yard was getting a built-in swimming pool, or at least a woman-made lake!

The main water valve to the house was turned off, and I went to bed after brushing my teeth in Evian. The next morning, I called a plumber. His charming answering service person answered. I said, "You don't know me, and so far today, you don't want to know me. I haven't had a shower in 24 hours. I'm hoping you can help me." She began to laugh.

Assuring myself that help was en route, I went about my work. The plumber arrived. A nice, quick man who slid into the spider in-fested crawl space below my house, emerged muddy from head to toe and disappeared, promising he'd be back in half an hour with the missing length of pipe and some sort of valve.

I was cheerful. I gave him coffee. I was not suspicious in the least. When he hadn't returned in an hour, I called my new friend, who assured me he would soon be back. She apologized that I hadn't heard from him. Two hours later, I called again. She said she'd page him. Four hours later, no water yet, no sign of the plumber, I called again. She paged him again. He called and left me a message. "Sorry, I can't get the part. Can't get back there this week. Call someone else." Click.

All the charm in the world would not get me running water. Calling her and yelling would not get me results. I picked up the Yellow Pages and started dialing, nearly frantic. In 10 minutes, I had spoken to one monosyllabic man who had no interest in helping me, two people who were so busy they couldn't come out for at least a week, three women who took my name and number and swore someone would call me back instantly (still waiting), and, finally, one man who promised that for $79 he'd have someone take a look today and they'd give me an estimate on whether or not it was fixable. He added that perhaps I might need the whole house replumbed! (He's never been there, remember!)

The variety of ways I was treated reminded me that customers make a big decision from the first impressions I make, too. I was desperate for a plumber. At last, there's a plumber under the house right now, and I sure do hope he will fix it before he leaves. I don't want to write dirty books, but each of these companies decided not to build rapport with me, the customer. They didn't do what they said. I was stuck because I needed them; it was not a choice. The way they treated me gave me a strong negative impression.

Being charming or building rapport doesn't guarantee you the outcome you desire. It makes the transactions move forward more smoothly. If the first plumber had returned as promised, I'd be telling a very different story. But by creating a nice little moment of laughter with his assistant, at least the dreadful situation started off more positively.

People are naturally suspicious of others. I wonder if the man under my house is going to agree with the other company and say, "Lady, you need your whole house replumbed." I wonder if this guy is going to do a good job. My customers wonder if I will really sell their books to a publisher. The publisher wonders if I am over-selling the client's abilities and the book will be a dud, selling next to no copies.

Because of fiascos we've all had (like my plumbing pity party), people are suspicious. You need to take overt, positive, dramatic action to assert your good nature, your reliability, and your honesty. The easiest way to do this is to create rapport with the other person. The next chapter talks about the critical importance of honesty and trust and how it can transform your negotiations.

In Summary

A little grease oils the wheel. Why be squeaky if you don't have to be?

CHAPTER 16

Honesty and Trust

"Too often we take our own credibility for granted and don't make a buttressing effort. It's almost as if we assume everyone will consider us as straightforward and honest as we know we are. But a safer assumption for you to make is your counterpart will be just as concerned with whether you are bluffing as you are with whether he is. Don't forget, in these environs, a certain amount of suspicion and doubt come with the territory."
—James C. Freund,
Smart Negotiating

Have you ever walked into a place of business and got the feeling they were just plain dishonest? Have you ever sat down with a salesperson and felt like they were trying to "pull a fast one" on you? Sure, those kinds of places close some business. After all, there's a sucker born every minute.

But those are also the businesses best known as "fly-by-nights"— ones that have to escape angry customers and bill collectors by disappearing under cover of darkness.

The opposite is true, too. You can probably remember a purchase that you made when the sales professional took the time to connect with your real needs. She spent time explaining and perhaps explaining once more the elements of the product that were specific to your needs.

In journalism school at Arizona State in the very early 1980s, needing to pay school bills, I held several jobs at the same time. I found work at this newfangled place called a "health club." There were a few already in the greater Phoenix area, but this one was built in an old grocery store. There was a huge carpeted area with dozens of free weights and ugly, clanky exercise machines. The men who mostly frequented the gym had gigantic muscles they couldn't use for any real effort and brains curiously shrunken by use of chemicals.

My job was to sell health club memberships to mid-40s housewives and the occasional recently dumped male who came in to try to look like the muscle heads with minimal effort.

We had an aerobics area, which was in the middle of the machines and a large outdoor pool someone had put in the old parking lot of the grocery store. There were also some cubicles for the trainers. I was given 10 minutes of training on the operation of all these machines, a 15 page book on muscle groups and the benefits of weight resistance, and five or six days of training on how to sell health club memberships.

At this club, called a "spa" (for no valid reason), we were selling annual memberships for $399. It was fair at the time, because our competition was way, way on the other side of town.

But if you pleaded, we could get it down to you and a friend for a year for the same $399. We could also get you two years for $399. If none of that worked, then we could get you the same year for $299, $199, or even $99. In fact, on slow days, my manager would let you have three years for the $99. (FYI: This is *not* how health clubs work anymore!)

Now, the entire principle of health clubs is "attrition." As much as it seems untrue from their brochures these days, the principle is the people who sign up won't show up most of the time. Can you imagine 2,000 members all showing up the same day at the same time? The club would burst! So we could sell as many memberships as possible, and just allow human nature—and a love of pigging out—to take care of the rest.

I was 18 years old and I couldn't imagine what these pudgy women had been through that caused them to let themselves go. So I used the script they gave me, and if they countered my offer of $399, I first tried to intimidate them. If that failed, I'd tell them in a whisper that I'd see if I could get them a special deal because I liked them and really believed in their commitment to lose weight, get in shape, whatever phrase they had used themselves on the tour.

I didn't really see what a scam the whole place was until years later. But I do remember wise customers who saw it as a scam. More often than not, they overheard the salesperson in the next room offer someone else the same membership at one of our cheaper prices. Or they had a friend who had gotten two years for $99. Or they suspected we were not being honest.

I left the club after two semesters at school. I heard it went out of business a year later, but that the man who had begun it had made a fortune. As I matured, I began to see how unfair and unkind what we were taught to do really was. I've also been the customer in situations like that, ones in which I know the bottom line isn't the bottom line but rather what they think they can sell me something for, based on the quality of my watch or handbag or car. It feels icky both ways. And in a more aware society, it's a death knell in a negotiation to lose the trust of another person.

It's All About Me, Me, Me!

Lisa Johnson, who we mete in Chapter 15 sells accessory lines all up and down the east coast. Lisa says this about building trust:

"I always look at the big picture. So many people are trying to sell, sell, sell as much as possible. Of course the client won't buy from them again, because the representative sold everyone too much or sold the same thing to everyone on the street. They were just interested in their own gain, not the customer's.

"I'm almost too honest with my clients. I try to sell them a little less than I should. I tell them, 'I would prefer you to call me back every week and want more, otherwise next season you won't buy from me at all because I oversold to you.' Once you mess up with them, they won't but from you again. You've lost their trust and you never get that back.

"Good negotiation is all about the level of trust. I think establishing trust comes from approaching people in a professional manner. You must respect their time. I ask, 'Did I reach you at a bad time? Let me call you back.' They know I'm right there, being considerate of their time. It's not about what I want; it's about it being good for them. That's the only way.

"I also always try to set up an appointment, and then they expect they are going to see me. In my business, you can just barge in on people, but I find that if you respect the other person, their attitude, their time, their space, their personality, you get a lot further. They trust and like you more.

"For instance, if you start to joke and they aren't laughing, you have to respect their professional attitude, their personality, who they are. I am a controlling person but I try to recognize when I'm with them not to be the controlling person. It works better. They trust me."

Establishing Trust

Trust is a critical factor. Modern buyers can "sniff out" dishonesty or unfair sales tactics, like those used in the health club industry 25 years ago. A business or professional who negotiates without being trustworthy is limiting themselves and their time in business.

Some of the smartest ways to establish the customer's trust and maintain it are:

- Tell the truth about your product without hyperbole.
- Offer a fair price.
- Have a generous return policy. Most people will never use it, and it makes it clear you stand behind your product.
- Look people in the eyes when speaking to them.
- Shake hands firmly before the real negotiation begins.
- Be clear in advance about what you need and want.
- Be sure to have done your homework so you know their "wiggle room" and your own.
- Be respectful of their time. Make the appointment and be prompt.

- ♣ Be courteous and calm at all times.
- ♣ Keep a level head. If you love what they're selling or you're starved for the commission on what your selling, and it shows, they've got you and they know it.
- ♣ Write down everything you agree to at once and provide a copy of it to them as soon as possible, ideally before they leave.
- ♣ Connect on a personal level. People buy from people they like and trust.
- ♣ Don't say more about the deal than you need to say to close the deal.
- ♣ Shut up and let the customer talk when you want to know how it's going.

Honesty *Is* the Best Policy

Carrie Lincoln, the stationery saleswoman, says, "I think they trust me to give them material that will sell. They know I will recommend things that work best for their stores. If they pick something bad, maybe I'll tell them not to buy something. Honesty always pays off. It is good business, you know. The more honest you are, the more honesty is going to come back to you. The orders come back, too!" she says, laughing.

"My honesty may be what works best for me. I think it is, actually. I also think I'm fun to deal with. I laugh, I tell jokes. I think they think I'm a nice break from their day, you know, dealing with customers and toner and reams of copy paper and stuff. I sell good stuff. I'm successful because I work hard, and I tell the truth.

"I really get to know people, too. When you're honest with them, and they trust you, getting to know them just sort of happens. Some days, I will call a client and they say, 'I was just thinking I should call you!' I may be psychic or something, or it may be just knowing the way it goes after 11 years. Or maybe, just maybe, it's that I've been 'let inside' their minds because I proved myself."

"The other thing is that I honestly believe in the companies for which I work. I sell good stuff, and I and the company stand behind it. That's important. People want to know that you trust the product, they can trust it, and their customers can trust it."

Money-Back Guarantee, No Questions Asked

If you are the consumer of a product are offered a 100-percent money-back guarantee, how much does that increase your confidence in the product? About 100 percent, if you're like most people.

The purpose of a guarantee is for the company to assert to total strangers—its customers—that it is so certain of the benefits of the product or service that it will stand behind it even to the point of refunding your money.

Mail order catalogs, infomercial products, and many other companies offer a money-back guarantee. Most larger products come with repair/replace guarantees or warranties. The purpose is to help customers feel confident in their purchases.

In California, we have a "lemon law" that even allows for the return of defective cars if they are found to be "lemons" within a certain period of time. I once had a Toshiba laptop that went back for service six times in its first four months with me. They eventually just replaced it, right after I lost my temper at its constant defects. I lost a big part of four months of productivity because it was always in the shop being reformatted. I've owned half a dozen Toshiba laptops, but that one, well, it was a real lemon.

As a provider of a good or a service, you want to offer a guarantee. As a consumer, you want to take products that guarantee your satisfaction. As a negotiator, you should consider guaranteeing your performance or product. It will make the whole deal a lot easier for the other party to sign.

Did you know that the "shipping and handling" charge assessed to items bought via mail order actually covers the seller's cost of goods? That's why it never gets refunded. Small though it may seem, that little "handling fee" is typically the actual wholesale price the retailer paid for the item. When you are thinking of arguing to return something to a mail order company, realize that the money spent on shipping and the hard-to-pin-down "handling fee" aren't likely to be coming back your way.

The Case of the Missing Tapes

I have a lot of friends and clients who are on infomercials or work in that industry. The true story I'll tell you here will illuminate for you why you always, always want to offer a performance guarantee when you negotiate a product or service.

A friend sells an information package on his infomercial. Buyers get a whole bunch of tapes or CDs, as well as documents, forms, books, and similar merchandise. It's meant to be like a home study course.

His company packages and sells thousands of these every day, at almost $200 per package. He sells everything with a 100-percent money-back guarantee, exclusive, of course, of shipping and handling.

As an experiment, a few years ago his company packaged—shrink-wrapped and packaged—25 sets of its product *without* the audio tapes. (This was before CDs). Everything else was in place, but the molded plastic containers that held 12 or 18 or 20 cassettes were completely empty.

What do you think happened?

Nothing.

Six months later, *one* customer called to report her tapes were missing. They were FedEx'ed to her at once. The other customers were never heard from!

A guarantee costs a company nothing, and can make the customer that much more comfortable in negotiations.

Imagine what would happen if home sellers were completely honest. If they gave you a 20-page list of all the things they hate about their home, all the things wrong with it. You might see some of the following:

- The plumbing backs up when you have more than four guests.
- The neighbor's dog barks around the clock.
- The water heater will need replacing this year.
- We cut some corners and the light switch upstairs doesn't connect to anything.

Now what would happen if they sold you the house and *guaranteed* that everything they had disclosed was true, and that there was nothing they didn't disclose that could annoy you—or they guaranteed they would fix it, repair it, and replace it, for a year, or 10.

Who wouldn't take a deal like that?

Apply this principle to negotiations. **The seventh principle is to stand by your product, service, or word.** Can you guarantee your product, your service, your performance? What can you add to make the other party more comfortable, more trusting of your honesty?

I decided to offer a 100-percent guarantee on everything my company does. I know we perform well, and it makes the negotiation simple. When the other party gets to an impasse and really can't decide, I say, "And then, of course, we guarantee our work."

It immediately moves them in my favor. And how many times has anyone taken me up on the guarantee? Once someone returned a $20 cassette tape on how to get published. Why? He changed his mind after listening and decided to be a screenwriter instead.

In Summary

If the people whom you give, buy, and sell to can't trust you, you won't be successful for long, if at all. If you don't trust the people who are trying to do business with you, walk. Be a woman of your word—and expect the same high standard from others.

CHAPTER 17

Scenario Planning

"The will to win is important,
but the will to prepare is vital."
—Lou Paterno,
former Penn State head football coach

Scenario planning can really help you plan your whole negotiation in advance, especially if you're feeling a little nervous. You can practice and prepare for eventualities that may occur and it will make you feel more confident, and confidence is such a huge factor in success.

By planning what might happen, what you'll say, what you'll do, and so on, you create a "game plan." It's like those coaches who draw with Xs and Os in locker rooms. Having a strategy makes you comfortable and confident, and is the final component in impeccable preparation. At this point in the book, you've learned enough about the potential variables and important elements to be ready to map out a logical sequence.

One technique that works is *role-playing*. You actually have someone else play the role of the person with whom you are negotiating. The challenge, at least in my experience, is that the other person with whom you are role-playing usually doesn't know what the other party is likely to say. Also, using pets for role-playing is never a useful idea. Your cat has no idea what your boss will say when you ask for a raise!

The "Train Your Brain" Game

I suggest and prefer a technique called *Mind Mapping*. Invented by Tony Buzan, Mind Mapping is allegedly based on the way your brain thinks. The simple techniques became so amazingly popular, and helped so many people reach clarity in decision making, preparation, and other functions of the brain that the system is now world-famous. The core premise is that your brain thinks in pictures, not straight lines of words (like in books). Think hieroglyphs vs. newspaper columns. Children draw pictures before they write words.

Mind Mapping is worthy of your time to study. But to simplify it for this book, you will start by just drawing a plain old circle. In the circle write the name/subject of the negotiation.

Next draw "arms" from the circle, connecting to other circles.

For a simple negotiation, you might have one large central circle, and then others as they occur to you. Around each of these secondary circles, you will want to write the issues that influence the negotiation.

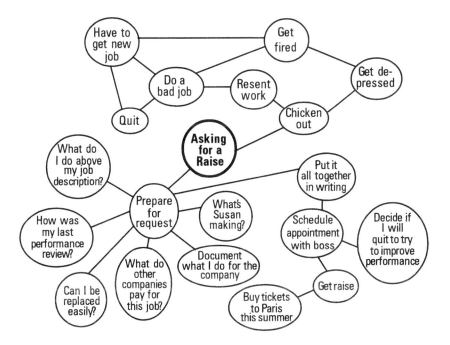

Creating a Mind Map helps you see what you need to prepare and what the potential outcomes are as well as their potential effect on you and your life. It also helps you visually "fill in the blanks." In the previous example, the person asking for a raise might also want to bring in statistics showing how customer service has improved, money has been saved, or a clutch of letters from clients complimenting her on her performance, demeanor, service, or other valuable contribution to the company's well being.

This scenario also helps you think calmly and rationally about the potentials, and helps you decide how much confidence you have in this negotiation. If the woman in our sample cannot prove she is of more value to the company, she may choose to "chicken out" and not negotiate for a raise at all. That leaves her with clear options, but she can also choose to improve her performance in preparation for the day she can be worth that raise in the boss's mind.

By laying it out objectively, it takes the fear and emotions out of a negotiation. It also helps you see how things can go, and be prepared for each eventuality.

How You Show Up at the Party

You get to the social event right on time, a dinner party at a friend's house. She's invited quite a crowd. Nearly 20 cars line the street as you pull in. You are wearing your best dress, your hair looks as good as it is ever going to, your makeup is perfect. Your escort, however, canceled at the last moment. You don't know what his plans are for the evening. He was evasive on the phone, even somewhat brisk with you. He sounded distant, remote. Your body shows up at the party, smiling charmingly, but your heart is somewhere else.

We all know the feeling of being in two places at once. Working mothers experience this when their child is home sick and they are in a board room listening to someone drone on and on about growth strategies or widget production graphs.

Men (especially those who play sports) learn to "get their head in the game." This training comes in handy in business. They seem to actually have an argument with us in the morning, go to work, have a great day, come home, and have actually forgotten many of the details of that whole morning's episode. We don't tend to have the same skill. We're more likely to be worried about it during the day, call him at the office to "clear the air," talk to a compassionate friend at lunch to determine what to do, and nearly dread the encounter coming up when we get home.

There's a famous saying: "Your attitude determines your altitude." This means, on one level, that what you expect out of life you tend to get, but even more importantly, in a negotiation it means you must get your attitude right to get the negotiation right.

You simply must learn the skill of compartmentalization if you are going to negotiate with power. If your making this deal is crucial to the rest of your life and will stop foreclosure on your home, the other party absolutely *must* have no clue of that.

Your job as a negotiator is to appear balanced, positive, upbeat, and, above all, unattached to the outcome.

How do you achieve this? Simple. You have taken the steps outlined in this and the preceding chapters to make yourself ready. You are well informed about the other side. You have chosen a good location for the negotiation. You've thought of possible scenarios and planned how you will handle them. You've done all you can. It's show time now. The curtain rises. There you are, ready to go and dazzle them with your brilliance and the excitement you share for the deal you are about to create. You're ready now. Let the show begin!

CHAPTER 18

Educating the Client

Good teaching is one-fourth preparation and
three-fourths pure theatre."
—Gail Godwin,
American novelist

Just like you have lots to find out about the person/company you
are negotiating with, they want to know a little something about you
and your company. You won't be the only one doing a little investigation. They'll be checking you out, too.

It might be your credit record, it might be what kind of car you
drove to their store, but if the negotiation is big, the other party will be
trying to find out as much about you as you do about them. They can
see your Website, they can look at your fancy watch, or listen to your
powerful voice. They can check Dunn & Bradstreet. But sometimes,
they want to know more. The best source of information on you is
you! But sometimes, women are trained to be "meek" or "polite" or
"humble." When's the last time you asked a man about something
he'd accomplished and he didn't puff out his chest and regale you
with a story of his incredible skill, talent, or cleverness? For the sake of
negotiations, it's a good thing to toss in a well-timed, even pre-planned
"pot sticker"—that nourishing little tidbit they can chew on while you
pretend it was unintentional.

Resting on Your Own Laurels

My colleague Cindi sits across the desk from me. We're discussing which authors I represent who have infomercial potential. I remark that one of the men is a genius, a natural, but that he is convinced he's the center of the universe and the rest of us are here to serve him. Personally, I always find such personalities tiresome.

Cindi says, "Then I want to talk to him!" I am shocked. I ask her why. She says something that changed my perspective forever. She said, "This business has a lot of ups and downs. We need people who always think they're right, who always think they will soon come out on top. In fact, those are the only ones who survive."

Musing this still, two weeks later I'm at lunch with a bright and hopeful young woman. She's determined to get a book deal, an infomercial deal, a radio show, a miniseries, a one-woman play, and probably her own penthouse suite in midtown Manhattan. She intrigues me. She talks without stopping for more than an hour. I am mesmerized by her attitude, not by her words. Suddenly conscious, she asks me a question. I take a moment to respond, surprised to be included in her soliloquy. Before I can respond, she has catapulted herself down another line of thought, talking furiously, eagerly, about all her exciting plans.

When my ears stop ringing, I think about her verve, her confidence, her nearly endearing enthusiasm. Perhaps it was slightly inflated because she was nervous being with me, but more likely, she's like this all the time.

I begin to wonder when I stopped being like these people. When did I stop thinking I was the center of the universe? What would it feel like to wake up as these people, believing each moment of every day is there for your benefit?

Brian Tracy, noted motivational speaker and author, says to repeat 100 times a day into the mirror, "I like myself!" I wonder how many people do that. Would that turn us all into the woman at my lunch date?

I live in Malibu, a little rural, country town stuffed to the brim with celebrities and the people who profit from them. I've observed some extraordinarily pushy behavior, and I've also observed some amazing philanthropy. Mel Gibson has children matriculating with my daughter and frequently and generously contributes to the school.

I saw Brad Pitt make good on owing 48 cents at the copy store. Pierce Brosnan's tenderness toward his late wife was legendary in town.

I've also met a thousand want-to-be celebrities. Rude, abrasive, putting on airs. Annoying, demanding, difficult. Did the "big stars" have to go through that period, too, before they became big? Did they all do long monologues on their dreams?

It appears to me that treating everyone graciously and dropping a few gentle hints about your credentials is the most elegant way to make sure your audience knows who you are. How else can they determine your qualifications?

When you enter into a negotiation, sometimes the person across from you doesn't know who you are. Not in the sense of, "Do you know who you're speaking to? You'll never work in this industry again!" (Although there may be a time for that.) But, more importantly, to understand that you respect them and they need to respect you, as well.

> We confide in our strength, without boasting of it;
> we respect that of others, without fearing it.
> —Thomas Jefferson

The easiest way to gain respect is to give it. The easiest way to maintain it is to give it and also drop a few gentle hints about your credentials along the way. I frequently tell people I train to be on radio and television interviews to say, "Good question, Jim. Someone in my seminar last month asked the same thing. The best answer I've found is...."

The astute listener just learned that the media guest is also a seminar leader. The guest didn't clobber the audience with it. He or she laid it out there, for those who have ears to hear. In other words, anyone interested. Of course, you have to tell the truth.

In a negotiation, you might say, "You know, I respect your concern about that. The top negotiation team at a *Fortune* 500 company we work with asked the very same thing...."

I often use something such as, "I was so happy! My last three authors to graduate from our author development program went on to get book deals. That sure makes me feel proud of our system." Or I'll tell a nervous prospective author, "You know, I felt the same way when my first book came out in 1991. But now, 27 published books later, I know that...."

Try these:

"When I was presenting a paper in front of Congress once, I ran into a very similar situation...."

"Back before I started this company, when I was still VP of what's now my largest competitor...."

"You know, seven long years ago when I started this company, before we'd helped so many people get the widgets of their dreams, I couldn't believe how many people trusted us without a track record."

"I really appreciate the customer service you're giving me today, Susan. Before we transferred to Verizon, we were with Pacific Bell for nearly seven years. They had all 10 of our business accounts. I told my boss we should switch to you guys, and I'm glad we did. Now, about the recent billing error...."

You can easily adapt these phrases to reflect what message you need to convey.

The secret is "read between the lines." The message you are conveying has at least two meanings in every case. This is a subtle art that can best be used in a negotiation where things are starting to go a little off course, before they get too far down the road.

You need to create some of these "subtle" phrases now, in advance of needing them. Think about the situations in which you are negotiating. Even if you think they already know your credentials, it's helpful to gently remind them you didn't just fall off the turnip truck. You're a respectable, accomplished professional and you deserve good service, their trust, their business, their agreement, and so on.

In Summary

Who you say you are is every bit as important as how you show up. Read your own press releases, and make sure the other party does, too!

CHAPTER 19

A Tree Falling
in the Forest

"There's nothing that keeps its youth,
So far as I know, but a tree and truth."
—Oliver Wendell Holmes (1809-1894),
The Deacon's Masterpiece, 1858

A critical tool, an invaluable resource for negotiation, and one in which women tend to excel, is **listening.** In order to understand what you want, you have to listen to your heart and mind. In order to listen to what the other party wants, you have to listen to their words and learn to hear their heart speak.

Listening is something we all *think* we do just fine. Ask the people closest to you how you are at listening, especially your kids. Chances are, if you're human, there's room for improvement.

"Being willing to change allows you to move from
a point of view to a viewing point—a higher,
more expansive place from which you can see
both sides."
—Thomas Crum,
author of *The Magic of Conflict*

We tend to hear other people through our own filters. In my first news reporting class at university, the professor said to imagine a gunman coming into the student union, screaming obscenities, firing shots, then running out the back door a few moments later.

As journalists, we were then to imagine having to report this event. He taught us:

"When you interview the first person, they will explain what they saw: 'The gunman was about 20 years old, with brown hair and a red sweatshirt on. He was screaming in some foreign language.'

"The second person you interview was standing by the soda machine. She says, 'Oh! It was terrible! Two gunmen came in yelling in some foreign language. I heard the shots and people were screaming! There was noise everywhere, and that guy over there who got shot was yelling in pain.'

"The third person you interview will describe the blood splattered on the walls; another will tell you there were two gunman, explain which language they were yelling, and what their issues were; and a fifth will tell you the make of the blue jeans the lone gunman was wearing."

The point our teacher was trying to make—and which proved itself true in the years I was a reporter after school—was that everyone has a different opinion. Everyone sees it from their own perspective. If there were five witnesses, there are six truths—the sixth being the collective.

My daughter comes home from school in tears and tells me about some mean girl who said something unkind. I am not hearing my daughter's story but not just because I am not talking while she is. I am thinking about Becky of Cottonwood, Ariz., the terror of my own middle school years. She made my life miserable for years with her lies and gossip. My latent anger for Becky resurfaces as anger toward the child who has hurt mine and is thus repeating the cycle. I am thinking about calling the principal, calling the child's mother and father. I'm thinking about enrolling my daughter in karate. By the time she's finished talking, I certainly understand. I understand something must change and I must change it.

I leap in to offer a solution, mother bear ready to defend her cub. My daughter is surprised. She says, "Mom, it's okay now. Rachel and I apologized to each other. I was just going to ask you if she can come over this weekend for a sleepover."

You've probably heard that we can listen three times faster than the average person can talk. That gives our brain plenty of time to guess where the other party is going, go there, make a decision, come back to their words in real time and wait for them to finish so we can respond. (What took you so long?)

Listening in business is a learned skill. It means that you don't value the appearance of "thinking on your feet." Instead you value the speed at which the other person communicates, and like my journalism professor taught, you get the whole story.

To complicate things further, people communicate on many of levels. They communicate with their bodies, their eyes, their words, even unseen communication. A good negotiator gets the "lay of the land" before she jumps into the negotiation.

Your job is to figure out what the person really means. They may be lying. They may not know what they want. They may be bluffing—which is a very common negotiation tactic. You need to read all the signals, hear the words, and form the best possible questions to determine the accuracy of your assessments.

To make this extremely easy, here are the simple rules of listening in a negotiation situation.

Listening Skill One

Try to listen before you get to the negotiation to find out on the phone, if possible, what the other side's primary concerns are. I often write down notes as I'm chatting with someone I expect to negotiate with soon. At the actual negotiation, you want to listen even more attentively, and pay attention to body language.

I try to always listen on two levels: what they say they want, and what they really want.

For instance, many hopeful authors go on and on about how they feel in their hearts that their book will change the world. I listen for a while, encouraging them to empty by saying "Uh-huh" or "Yes" or "That's so noble of you" while they tell me their spiel. Once they are certain I'm convinced that their noble motives are all that drive them day and night, they will usually immediately tell me (or I will gently ask) what they really want out of it: fame, money, and free time to write are the three most common real reasons people want to create a book. The more "change the world" types are usually the most difficult to deal with because they expect inordinate fame, money, and the resultant free time to come instantly and rarely are they open to the idea that their core book concept needs strengthening.

Listening Skill Two

Repeat their exact requests as questions, to ascertain that you comprehended. Make sure you use their language or it will sound different to them.

Imagine this:

A 40-something woman carrying a few extra pounds walks into a health club and wants to sign up for the membership special. The salesperson is trying to listen. He's a buff young man in his 20s.

She says, "I've been thinking about doing this for years, but I just never had time before."

"That's great!" he says. "You know, we're open 24/7 to fit into your schedule."

She wasn't thinking about the times the gym was open when she made her comment. Instead she meant that her kids were too small and her work schedule too hectic to afford her the time to get away, but it doesn't matter. She's now thinking about the 24/7 schedule and whether or not she'll really come as often as she hopes she will, considering her commitments. But she's still on track. He doesn't know he threw her into thinking about her still rather hectic life; he thinks he overcame her objection to not having time. After all, he has no kids, no wife, no house payments, and coming to the gym is his job.

He asks her, "What's your primary motivation for coming to the gym?" He's been taught to ask this question by some poor sales trainer who thinks there are stock questions for every pitch.

She says, "I just really decided to get in shape. I've noticed my metabolism is slowing down and I feel tired a lot of the time. Of course, it could be three kids, two dogs, and a full-time job!" She laughs at her own joke.

He doesn't hear her joke because he can't imagine what's funny about all that stuff she said. All he heard—the moment his brain left the conversation—is when she said she wants to get in shape. So he says, "This is the right place to be! We can get you looking hot in just a few months, especially if you work with one of our personal trainers. For a small extra fee...."

She doesn't want to look "hot." Her 16-year-old looks hot. Hot is not on her priority list. At this moment, it's going to take more salesmanship than he probably has to bring her smoothly to the close of their negotiation. It all happened because he didn't listen to her real needs, he failed to put himself in her situation, and when he did, it was based on his youth and inexperience.

Chances are she'll sign up anyway, despite him. But she won't feel comfortable at the gym, or she'll find herself "too busy" to show up a few months from now, gain a few pounds, and let her guilt swamp her plans for fitness. He planted those thoughts in her mind: *The gym is a place to come to look hot. They're open 24/7 so you have no excuse. If you don't show up you're a loser.*

In a negotiation, it's critical to listen to the other party's real comments and not filter them. *Hear* them.

He should have said, "How would you describe the changes in your metabolism?" or "What do you mean by 'feeling tired'?" That way, she could have elaborated on the real issues that are bringing her to the gym, not the desire to look hot.

The Power of Questions

Jeanne Coughlin, a Cleveland business leader, says, "A practical point is the more questions you are asking, the better place you are in, the stronger your position is. When you start talking is when you move into trouble with things. When you're talking, you can easily give too much information. You also stop learning, and certainly stop getting information. Listening and asking questions will also give you some space to regroup, ask a question, and take the time they are talking to regroup some more."

Asking questions puts you in control of the situation again. It causes the other party to think and respond. It also force the other party to show their hand.

Listening Skill Three

Once you understand the question, repeat it as a statement.

Mrs. Dunmire says, "I really need you to have the bathroom remodeled before Christmas. Can you guarantee that?"

Mr. Jackson says, "You know, M'am, we'll do our best."

Mrs. Dunmire, who is not only a reader of this book but a shrewd woman, realizes he hasn't answered her question. She says, "I need a guarantee in the contract that you will be done by December 23rd. Will you agree to that?"

Mr. Jackson now must think about whether he is actually prepared to perform. He says, "Sure. That's no problem."

Mrs. Dunmire, who has been through this sort of thing before says, "So we agree that you will put into the contract that you will be done by December 23rd. If you are not for any reason, I will expect a $250 per day rebate for each day past the 23rd that it remains undone."

Mr. Jackson now must determine which conditions can be met and which cannot. He's smart, too, and he's got a good crew. He is 99 percent certain he can meet her request. He says, "Yes, we'll put it in the contract that we will be done by December 23rd. And if we're not, and it is through no fault of our own—you change your mind, or we can't get approval on the plans—then yes, we'll refund you $250 for each day we go past the deadline."

Mrs. Dunmire would have been able to listen on two levels and watch. If Mr. Jackson started yanking his earlobe, darting his eyes, or crossing his legs, arms, or hands during this conversation, she would have seen that he is not confident that he can complete the job promptly and is probably lying to her. Those body signals all indicate lying, hiding something, or closing off, respectively.

Likewise, if Mrs. Dunmire is asking these things in a threatening, angry manner—her hands are on her hips, her voice is elevated or shrill, or she's glaring at him—Mr. Jackson should think twice about taking on such a sure-to-be-high-maintenance customer.

By being completely clear, repeating the question, and watching one another's body language, they can reach a fair agreement. Both sides trust the other to perform, not merely because of a contract, but because of the people behind the contract.

Through long and hard experience, we all learn a contract is only as good as the people behind it. If Mrs. Dunmire has the intent to overwork Mr. Jackson's crew and make unreasonable demands, the contract will be useless to them both. If Mr. Jackson is planning to take the down payment and not show up for work until December 20th, the contract will do no good.

The legal hassles of fighting such things in court and the emotional and mental drain of such situations makes it a far better decision to choose your negotiation and business partners wisely. Mr. Jackson can find another client who is calmer if he suspects she will be obstreperous. Mrs. Dunmire can find a contractor who is more confident with his scheduling if she suspects he is not.

Listening Skill Four

Asking is power. Even if you are clearly the underdog in a negotiation, such as when petitioning a boss for a raise, you are in the power position when you are asking questions.

The following is interchange between Linda, who wants a raise, and her boss, Ms. Simms:

"Ms. Simms, I've put together some data for you on how the cost of office supplies has dropped since I began working for this company. May I show it to you?"

Linda is currently in control of the conversation. Her clear, benefit-oriented question is sure to elicit a favorable response.

"Certainly, Linda." She reads the simple document. "That's excellent. I had no idea. How did you save this money?"

Ms. Simms is currently in control of the conversation. She's the one with the question.

Linda says, "The first thing I did was get the lock fixed on the supply room door. A lot of things were leaving so fast that I couldn't keep track of them. Then we'd either have to buy at the last minute and pay rush fees, or we'd have four of something because everyone in the office would order it.

"The other thing I did was to organize everything on the shelves. I put together and keep a list of the supplies—an inventory. I write down who takes what and when. As I watched the patterns, I was able to order so that we always had enough of the items we would need.

"And perhaps most importantly, I asked everyone here to sign in with me when they take something. Do you see where it shows how this alone has saved almost $500 per month?"

Linda has shown Ms. Simms the extent of her action and her foresight and has spoken clearly and logically. She has returned the conversation to her favor by answering and then asking a new question.

Ms. Simms looks at the number highlighted by Linda in yellow on the paper. She says, "This is excellent work, Linda. Thank you!"

This is a dead end. It's a skilled use of language Ms. Simms has been trained to use to stymie Linda into acknowledging the thank you, being happy for the praise, and forgetting her objective, which Ms. Simms probably knows is coming. Remember the first chapter where we talked about all the forces aligning for your good? What Linda does now will determine her success.

Linda says, "You're welcome. It was interesting to see how much can change with just a little organization. Now I'm working on organizing the office library and the use of company equipment off-site. I expect to report on that to you by the end of the month."

Linda pauses, because the use of artful silence is a gift few can master. Beat. Beat.

If Ms. Simms doesn't jump in to offer praise and maybe even the raise, Linda is going to do it herself. She doesn't, so Linda does.

"Ms. Simms, my work here is saving the company money, making things more efficient for the entire staff, and helping to accomplish our stated goal of reducing costs and raising revenues this year. In light of my proven contributions, I am asking for a raise of $2.50 per hour."

She didn't say, "I'd like to ask for a raise." or "I think I deserve a raise." or "I want a raise." She spoke forcefully. "I am asking..." is powerful statement between equals, and implies it's happening in the present moment, and thus must be dealt with right here, right now.

Ms. Simms may not agree instantly to $2.50 per hour more for Linda. Maybe she doesn't have the money. She may say she needs to think about it. (If she does, Linda should get her to agree to a specific date and time when they will conclude this conversation.) She may offer a counter. Let's examine that approach:

Ms. Simms says, "I can certainly see how your contributions have been valuable to this company, Linda. Thank you for your hard work and good ideas. I agree that you should get a raise for your efforts."

Ms. Simms is smart. She takes the invaluable pause. She's looking right at Linda to watch her reactions. Did she blossom when she praised her? Most management books teach managers that employees will do more for praise than a raise. Does Linda look nervous? Did she perk up when she said she agrees to giving her a raise? Should she ask Linda if something major is wrong in her life?

Linda's smart. She doesn't bite the pause. She sits there smiling, as if waiting for Ms. Simms to continue.

Ms. Simms, forced to answer because the ball was left in her own court, says, "I believe we can offer you $1.75 per hour more, starting next Tuesday. How's that?"

Linda is thrilled, but remains calm. She had hoped to get close to her expected amount.

And now, Linda will use the coup d'etat that only professional negotiators usually have the guts to use.

Linda says, "Oh, thank you! That's wonderful! I really appreciate it. And because we're talking about it, next month when I bring in the money-saving results from the office library and off-site equipment programs I'm creating, can we talk about the balance of the $2.50 per hour I requested?"

Ms. Simms sees a woman who is going places in the world. *She's smart, a self-starter and she's got guts*, Ms. Simms thinks to herself. *We need to make sure we keep her working for us. She's got management potential, too. Maybe I should recommend her for the training program.*

Ms. Simms says, "Of course, Linda. We'll talk then. Thanks for coming in, and for all your good work with the office supplies."

Both parties just won this negotiation.

Remember: You don't know what the other person is thinking. They will *never* tell you the whole truth. Linda doesn't know her display of negotiation skills set her far ahead of her peers in Ms. Simms's mind. Ms. Simms didn't know that Linda wants the extra money so she can go to night school and get more training for the job she really wants in management. But a happy convergence of needs created success for them both.

Using the Pause Button

Just like your remote control for the DVD player, your mouth also has a pause button. Just like you control the DVD, you can control the conversation. Once words are spoken they can never be rewound.

If you are about to yell, insult, scream, or say something hurtful to someone, hit the pause button.

If you are about to undersell yourself or oversell a product or service you know you can't deliver, hit the pause button.

If you are about to agree to something you know in your heart you completely don't want to do—whether it's chaperone the first grade field trip, work overtime, or take no for an answer at the returns counter, hit the pause button.

There's always time to regroup. Whether you need a few seconds, minutes, hours, or days, take the time you need to strategize your position and your real objection. Remember, it's all about what you really want. Get back in touch with that during the pause.

Will you win the battle but lose the war if you do or say what you are about to do or say?

What's your ultimate objective?

Is this a peach you want to pick, or a battle worth pitching?

The pause button diffuses all the words you were going to say in reaction and allows you to say the words you want to say from wisdom.

Verbal interchange and body language observance are important skills in any negotiation. To master body language skills, pick up a copy of Julius Fast's classic work *Body Language* (M. Evans and Co., 1970) and read *Instant Rapport* by Michael Brooks (Warner Books, 1990). There's a whole science behind these techniques worthy of study.

Meanwhile, watch your tongue and the other person's gestures. Listen for what he or she is really saying with his or her words, body, and heart. You have the gift of intuition as a birthright of your gender. Use it!

In Summary

She who asks the questions controls the conversation. Listening, pausing, and evaluating before you respond allows you to communicate from strength.

CHAPTER 20

What I Think You Said I Said

"When you speak...they don't respond to what you say; they respond to what they understand you to say."
—Nido Qubein, author/speaker
Achieving Peak Performance

In 1996, I had a management experience that changed my life forever. My most significant guru, a wise woman named Ernestine Fischer, facilitated a seminar up at a ranch/retreat near San Francisco. About 40 women attended with me.

The time on this ranch was grueling. We suffered physical deprivations in addition to going through extreme mental changes in a very short period of time. We stayed in decrepit multi-unit dormitories, rather like Native American longhouses. As a creature of comfort, I did not like the mattress, the room temperature, the wait for the bathroom, the cold running water, or, most of all, not having a moment of privacy in a room full of 40 other women.

But what I took home from this experience shook me to my core. By sharing it here with you, I trust that the power in the lesson Ernestine taught me will transform your life, and your negotiation and communication skills, as it did mine.

On the last day of the retreat, our leader announced our task for the day was to clean the dormitory. Having paid several thousand dollars for the hardship I was already enduring I was not enthusiastic about now cleaning. Nonetheless, we resolved to do it.

Ernestine set up the rules. We were not allowed to talk from 6 a.m. until sunset. Only the "boss" for the hour was allowed to talk, and we were broken into teams and each had to be the boss for a certain period of time. The rest of us had to simply obey, doing precisely and exactly what the boss told us to do. We were allowed to take her English only at face value. We were not allowed to think we understood what she said. When the task was complete, we were to stand or sit precisely where we were, without speaking or moving. Like robots.

It seemed simple enough. Ernestine gave us an example. She said the boss may say, "Mop this floor." If the boss said that, we were to do nothing but stand there until clearer instruction was given. The boss would have to be more clear. She'd have to say, "Fill this bucket with warm water and this particular detergent. Then, insert this mop, wring it out, and moving in such a pattern, mop the floor beginning in that corner...." And so on.

It was, of course, preposterous.

And humbling.

Regina was our boss in the third hour. A big, powerful woman, I admired her on a thousand levels already. I was delighted she was the boss. She strode into the kitchen where I had been stationed next to a messy toaster area. At nearly 6 feet tall, she made anyone look up to her. She smiled a tense smile, although she was finding being the boss hard.

"Wendy, clean this counter."

I did not move. I've cleaned 2,000 counters in my life, but that wasn't clear.

Regina snapped. It's a lot of pressure to keep 10 women busy for an hour. She screamed at me. "Dammit, Wendy! I want you to take each and every single one of these $#%&@ crumbs and put them in the trash."

She left. At her specific request, I began taking the toast crumbs one by one and placing them in the trash across the room. After 50 or so, it was a Zen experience. I was the boy in *The Karate Kid*. It was transcendental. Regina came back after close to 40 minutes, to check on my progress.

She started to yell and then had to laugh. "Oh! Each and every one! Oh, I never thought of that!" We both laughed.

I came home from the trip, heavily enmeshed in the crumb experience. I told my daughter, who was then 5 years old, to put her folded laundry in her room. At bedtime, there it was. Neatly stacked three inches inside her doorway. I demanded an explanation.

Big blue eyes stared up at me bewildered. "Mommy, you said to put it in my room. I did it."

Have you ever told a man a problem, hoping he would listen like a girlfriend, and then been surprised or annoyed when he launched into all the ways you could fix the problem?

Have you ever told a colleague or an employer one thing and watched them walk away thinking something entirely different?

Remember the telephone game at the sleepovers you went to when you were 10 years old?

Life *is* the telephone game!

You need to use a trick used by professional speakers, in all your important communication, but even more in your negotiation communications.

1. Tell them what you're going to tell them.
2. Tell them.
3. Tell them what you told them.

You think they'll hear your redundancy and think you're talking down to them? Guess again! Clear communication is the underpinning of strong negotiation skills. Read through this scenario for a real-life example.

I'm working a book deal with a Big 6 publisher (Random House, Simon & Schuster, Warner, and so on.)

The editor and I are about to begin negotiating the terms for the deal and what the author will be paid in advance and in royalties for the book.

I say, "Did I tell you that Jim may be about to sign an infomercial deal with Acme Infomercials?" *I've indicated what I'm going to talk about—in this case, it is repetitious and I know it, but I will use it because it is a major leverage point in the deal.*

Editor says, "Yes, that's great. That's a big factor in our decision."

I say, "When he signs the infomercial deal, we expect that you will be able to provide Acme with books at a discount that they can sell to the public directly when the show becomes successful." *I've just taken the infomercial into the tangible, I've made it real in the publisher's mind, and I've brought them into the picture. In short, I've just "told them what I want to tell them."*

The editor says, "Oh, of course! We did something similar with another author last year and it went really well. I'll put you in touch with our Special Sales director for that."

I say, "Great! Yes, I believe this infomercial deal is an important factor in your decision here. You're getting a great deal when you publish this author." *I've repeated myself, and more importantly, led her to think about it the way I want her to think about it. That it's a "great deal." And so it is.*

When you remember these three tips (listed on page 150), you will make sure all parties understand close to the same thing, and you will have also taken responsibility for shaping the emotional attachment the other party has to the deal in the first place.

Clarity is your responsibility. I tell my daughter when she's frustrated with being misunderstood that "Communication is the responsibility of the speaker." If the people with whom you are communicating don't understand you because you beat around the bush, didn't know what you wanted to say yourself, were thinking aloud, or just weren't paying attention, you will annoy and frustrate the people around you. Clarity is critical, and it's your responsibility!

Negotiating for
Better Employee Performance

Lucy Plyler, my high school friend who works in an influential role of handing out money for her county (for more information see Chapter 7) said, "At work I'm going over the head of someone who isn't refunding some money to us. I will go over her head if I have to.

"I try not to make it an unequal playing field. Even though I have the authority and the money, I don't like to come across as such. Our funding can be pulled just as quickly as we can pull theirs. I try to be compassionate. I don't like the feeling I get when the state warns us they might pull our funding. I look at negotiations and even the times I have to reprimand someone as more of a partnership, and I outline each party's responsibility.

"When I have to tell someone they aren't meeting expectations, I think it's most important to be very, very clear. We've only had to write two corrective action plans, which is pretty good. There were times when they didn't realize they were doing something they weren't supposed to be doing. Sometimes people don't. You have to *listen* as well as tell.

"I write them a clear note that says:

This is what you need to do to fix it.
And if it is not fixed, there will be consequences/
we can't be your partners anymore.

"Before I go talk to someone, I talk with our fiscal manager and some of our other staff members. Then we talk to the agency. We have all the information before we get there. We're prepared. Then we talk about it. I ask what their plans are, why they are behind, whether or not they need to change. I tell them, "Now would be the time to tell me if you're not doing something and you need to fix it." I don't want to learn later in the year that they weren't meeting their goals. I'm very direct. You have to be direct.

"It's true for personal stuff, too. I had work done on my car recently. When I took it to a tire place, I thought they should be able to take a tire off if they can put them on. He rotated my tires. When I went to pick it up, I looked and my alloy wheels were completely scarred! I went back inside, fuming. I was so mad! I love that car. The manager came out and looked at the wheels. I told him they weren't scratched when I dropped the car off. I told him he needed to do something about this—give me all new wheels.

"He said, 'It didn't happen here, you have 50,000 miles on this car.' I was so angry! I told him to talk to the mechanic and I'd get back with him on what he is going to do to fix it. I called him back that afternoon and he said the mechanic had used an Allen wrench and a screwdriver to fix them. That's what messed them up. I got all new wheels.

"Maybe he wouldn't have argued with my husband if he'd been there. Or they would have gone to speak to the mechanic right away. I don't know how the experience would be different, but I suspect it would have been. He probably thought I'd back down. I believe I got what I needed from those people at the tire store because I was very clear and I had followed through on what I said. I told him what he had to do to fix it, I told him how to get the information he needed to make the decision, I called back when I said I would, I held him accountable, and every time I spoke with him I was very, very direct. People respond to direct communication."

In Summary

Being clear in your communications is critical to success. You must enunciate, choose your words carefully, speak clearly, allow questions, speak in a moderate tone of voice, and pay attention to be sure your listeners "got" your point.

CHAPTER 21

The President of the Charisma Club

"Charm is a way of getting the answer yes without asking a clear question."
—Albert Camus, author (1913–1960)

A former girlfriend of mine (we'll call her Violet) is renowned among her pals for making friends with anyone she wants to. She just simply walks up to total strangers and strikes up conversations. It's an enviable skill.

Violet wrote a mediocre book that had poor sales. I met her just as the book's shelf life was coming to an end. We struck up a friendship, as everyone does with her. There are several things you notice first about Violet. She wears the absolutely strangest clothes ever seen on a human being. She earned literally tens of millions of dollars selling her company at a young age. And she is completely, utterly brilliant when she isn't completely, utterly nuts.

She met me for lunch in Philadelphia one winter day, about a year after we'd become pals. She was wearing a faux leather shirt, with a flashy silver and rhinestone metallic belt that Pat Benatar might have worn on stage long ago, with a long, brown wool skirt with three slits in it up to her panties, and thigh-high gold lamé boots. Over all this she wore a mink that was to die for.

I was fascinated, as always, by her bizarre fashion sense and her amazingly alert mind. But today she was full of excitement. She'd donated a bundle of cash to the president's campaign, and so she'd been invited to a dinner at the White House. She told me what she wore, which designer gown. I could only imagine the shoes and funky handbag she would have taken along with it, and the stares from the political wives as they watched this waif-like creature come in with her wispy blond hair, raucous laughter, and razor-sharp brain. She must have seemed like an alien there.

True to her form, Violet took a copy of her dying book to the White House and managed to squirm, wriggle, and maneuver her way next to the president himself. And that's not all. She gave him the copy of the book she'd brought, and got him to promise to read it. On top of that, incredibly, she even got his personal invitation to call him to discuss the book once he'd had time to read it.

Beyond all cognition, not only did she call the president and get through, but she actually was offered a volunteer position helping out on one of the committees. Can you imagine?

Today at lunch her story was full of her success. I sat incredulous, my lunch getting cold, my fork still sitting beside my plate, untouched.

I said, "What's he like?" She said, "He exudes charisma! You can feel he's in the room from one hundred feet away. He's *there* and it's a big thing. I've never been around anyone like that. You can disagree with the man's politics all you want, but if you're in the same room with him, you're going to like him."

I've watched Violet for years now. She's made friends with celebrities, leaders, producers, politicos, the big shots, big dealers, and jet set all over the world. I've tried to understand how she gets into the places she gets into, and how she creates instant camaraderie with people she meets. The irony is that the friendships she makes never last long. Ours was a long-term one in her life—we were buddies for a few years. The other women I knew or met through her rarely stayed in her world for more than two years.

In retrospect, having not met that former president myself, I see that it is Violet who is the queen of charisma. She's the one who can light up a room, whose brazen disregard for polite society or social custom makes her so iconoclastic she's compelling. She's a drama queen, for certain, but she pulls it off with a remarkable amount of style.

The skills Violet naturally has can come in handy for you. By being "just like everyone else," you remain unremarkable, common, nice. Like the Diane Keaton character says in *The First Wives Club*, "Everything I own is the color of furniture! I spend my whole life looking like a couch!"

Here's what I learned from Violet that can make you charismatic, too.

- Talk to people as if you've known them for 20 years.
- Treat everyone as an equal, and a friend.
- Be outrageous.
- Take chances. Put yourself out there for things in which you believe.
- Start more conversations with other people than they do with you.
- Network your way through a room by watching who most people gravitate toward. Walk straight up to that person, without waiting in line, and say something clever.
- Wear remarkable clothing or accessories. It gives people something to talk with you about.
- Be bigger than life.
- Be mysterious.
- Be generous.
- Be bold.
- Look people in the eye when you talk to them.
- Share "secrets" with everyone, even if they are not secrets.
- Bring everyone into your heart without distinction. Let them in more than most people let people in. You can always remove them later.
- See mutual advantage in every relationship.
- Learn something from the other person.
- Compliment the other person.
- Be sincere about your strengths and lavish in your praise of the other person's strengths.
- Remember gifts, trinkets, little touches go a long, long way in our world.
- Be an intellectual magpie—collect data about everything and everyone all the time.

- Keep current on fashion, stars, news—you never know when you'll need to have a conversation with someone about these topics.
- Don't be afraid to be you—you have nothing to lose.
- Stir up a little fascinating drama in your life—and share it freely.
- Flit cheerfully from point to point, idea to idea, until you land on something the other person is truly interested in. Then, let them do the talking.

The Human Touch

Women have yet another natural advantage when it comes to negotiations. We are usually trained in the arts of social niceties. Most professional women have an expensive stack of monogrammed or personalized note cards in their desks they use to thank, encourage, or help people.

By applying the human touch in the hurly-burly business world, you take a step back and send a clear message to the other party: You matter. What greater kindness than one person reaching out with gentleness and thoughtfulness to another?

As a woman, you can demurely show your human side to a male negotiation partner without it being considered as making an advance. He cannot do the same.

It's so simple, and so ultimately effective!

The meeting was delayed because one of the parties was out sick? Skiing injury? Fender bender? Jury duty? You are a smart negotiator. You dash off a kind, handwritten personal note expressing the appropriate sentiment and slip it into the mail.

It's her birthday, her daughter's high school graduation, she just got married, had a baby? Depending on the importance of the negotiation, of course you send a note, a card, flowers, or even a small, tasteful gift.

She's having a bad day? Send a pick-me-up bouquet.

She just closed a gigantic deal with another company? A bottle of champagne.

Using a client management program such as ACT! (*www.act.com*) helps you or your staff able to stay on top of the personal days important to people with whom you do business, as long as you remember to gather and input important data.

There's nothing like being kind, warm, considerate, and thoughtful to make negotiations more fun and smooth. Use your feminine skills and training to "bond" with other people, especially people who are important to you or your business future.

Susan Miller-Stanton, whose business revenues as an insurance broker have tripled in the past three years, sees it comes back tenfold. While I interviewed her for this book, she said, "I find that remembering their birthday, sending them a card, remembering they had a baby boy last month, things like that make you stand out from any other person that tries to sell them something or just do business with them. After all, it's about creating real relationships. It comes back, too. I have many customers who treat me very, very well. They feed me when I visit them, invite me over, they give me gifts, housewarming gifts, send me flowers. It makes business nicer when you can warm it up."

Grease of Human Kindness

As a kid, my family lived in Vail, Colo., for a year. I was bored and 12 years old, and soon got offered the job of babysitting the children of the restaurateur who lived next door. The children spoke only Japanese. I spoke only English. It was unfortunate from the beginning.

But because my father had a measure of leverage over the Japanese man, because he was the contractor in charge of the building's facelift, the man did me the honor of paying me $100 and loading me down with several unique gifts to thank me for watching his children on and off for a month. My parents were touched.

A decade later, a lovely Japanese woman came to America to visit us and meet me. She brought gifts for me and my husband and very generously spent two cheerful hours with us, despite the intense language barrier.

A decade after that, I came to know a Korean man named Rob. I watched in fascination as vendor after vendor cheerily called out his name, gave him impeccable service, and helped him meet his every whim. I'd never seen anything like it. Rob's father had been the single largest builder in Korea. He told me his father had taught him that business requires two things: that you ask and remember people's names, and that you "grease the wheels" a little. Rob always carried a thick stack of bills to "grease the wheels" of his life, and I have truly never seen such a masterful use of cash as a means of accomplishing any impossible task.

A few years later, I had the honor of working with a noted Chinese author. A gracious, poised, and very intelligent woman, I found myself slightly in awe of her. When she called upon me for services that were above and beyond my scope of business, I did so willingly, eager to help her. You cannot imagine my surprise when a few days later, a Louis Vuitton wallet arrived at my doorstep with her thanks.

I am seeing a parallel here. It may well be that Americans take umbrage and call out, "Bribe!" to people who "grease the palms" of those who help them. But we leave a tip after the meal, a backwards use of the original intention, which was "to insure promptness." Thus the name, "TIP." We seem to think that the good ol' Protestant work ethic is enough to make everyone leap to attend to our whims. Does it?

It seems to me that the Asian cultures may have it right. Perhaps by being kind, generous, and personable *in advance of good service,* good service is increased. Of course, discretion is always required. One wouldn't want to insult another by giving a gift before a deal was negotiated. But if that is always true, then why do men buy one another endless rounds of fine Scotch at business dinners, or play rounds of golf and then mysteriously end up with the deal?

In Summary

Just like your mom always said, to have friends you have to show yourself friendly. Use your charisma and some "friendship grease" artfully applied.

CHAPTER 22

Take
Massive Action

"You can express your passion in words, but
sometimes action is called for."
—Kate White, author,
*9 Secrets of Women
Who Get Everything They Want*

In *Dances With Wolves*, the leading female character firmly and clearly rejects the invasion of her people by standing with her fist straight up in the air. A strong, silent protest.

In America, at the beginning of the civil rights movement, Rosa Parks took strong action. She didn't write her congressman. She didn't pray extra hard. She didn't hope that things for African-Americans would get better or complain that they weren't. She may have done those things, too, but what she's known for is getting into a bus seat and not moving.

Sometimes, getting what you want requires you take an action. Not just say you want the deal, show them you want the deal. Follow up. Beg, plead, send roses. Send steak knives, barbecue sauce, and an oven mitt. Send lavender bath oil with a copy of your favorite novel. Do something!

Get big. Get serious. Get noticed. Two marketing geniuses of my acquaintance tell the story of how they got a big office supplies retailer to buy promotional copies of their self-published book—before it was really even written!

They claim they sent a balloon bouquet to the CEOs of the two target companies. No card attached. Next, they sent a big box of chocolates to those same leaders. Finally, they sent a chocolate engraved with the cover of their book, with a simple note asking that the CEOs take their call at a specified time tomorrow.

Do you think they took their calls?

You bet! They not only got their calls taken, but a few months later they had an order for 150,000 copies of their book! (That's more than most authors will sell in a lifetime!)

I've hired many people for the six companies I've owned. I've even been in charge of hiring senior staff for a metropolitan newspaper. Here's an example of how Josh and Carrie, two people who work for me now, got their jobs:

I posted a job ad in a few locations. Within three days, I'd gotten more than 400 responses by e-mail! Shocked at this overwhelming number, I began sifting through the piles of e-mails. The basic criteria I used were (1) whether there were typos in the cover letter (remember, we're a literary agency) and (2) whether they had any remotely related experience or evidence of interest (for example, an MFA or a degree in English or a published book of their own).

I quickly got down to eight ideal candidates. On Friday morning, I e-mailed all eight, telling them simultaneously they were under consideration for the position but they would not hear back from me for seven-10 days while I checked their references, and so on.

In 10 days, only two of the applicants responded to that e-mail with a courteous or hopeful note. In fact, only two responded at all. I hired them both!

Why? Because they took action. It signified to me that they were paying attention, that they were seriously interested in the job—not just spamming resumes around town. It showed that they were serious enough and confident enough in themselves to contact me directly.

Taking action is the single most critical factor in winning anything. You must enter to win! Just as you can't win a race if you don't run, you can't close the negotiation if you don't make the call. Half of success is merely "showing up." Just being there when no one else shows up, or few people make the effort, can make all the difference.

A girlfriend of mine, Iris Martin, sold her company for many millions of dollars. Incredulous that she should have created such magnificent wealth long before the age of 45 and all alone, I asked her how she did it. "I just wouldn't ever take no for an answer," she said. Iris frequently went to extreme lengths to get the meeting, get attention, and get the deal. She overwhelmed them with charm, kindness, and charisma. Her professional skills were able to shine when she finally had their attention. She took *massive action.*

> "If you want massive results,
> you MUST take massive action"
> —Anthony Robbins,
> *Awakan the Giant Within* (Free Press, 1992)

Taking action is critically important to your success. The amount of action to be taken is determined by the negotiation at hand and how bad you want it. If you want the CEO of a large company to meet with you, you'll have to put in some significant creative time and maybe some elbow grease to get that meeting. It's more than simply writing a memo or having your assistant call to request a meeting.

If you want your kid to clean her room, you'll have to take some action to enforce it. You catch more flies with honey than vinegar. Men know how to "butter up" the opponent in a sales and negotiation situation. They are trained to play golf, have a few drinks, hang out, and discuss "manly" topics. We complain about the "Old Boys' Network" but have we really tried to create a door for ourselves? Smart women figure it out.

This is not to say you need to play golf, but if the person with whom you are negotiating is a wine connoisseur, why not get the information on his favorite brand and send it to him *before the negotiation.* Can't do that because it would look like a bribe? Okay, sit there and hope it goes your way.

If the negotiation is postponed because the CEO's daughter is sick, why not send a cheery little get-well bouquet to the CEO's office—child appropriate, of course, with the teddy bear attached. You'll not only get the deal, you'll likely acquire a new friend.

The milk of human kindness needs to be liberally poured on everyone with whom you want to negotiate. By making allies before you enter the negotiation situation, you have minimized the chances that things won't go your way. You will have set yourself up as a "reliable, friendly sort of woman"—the people with whom we like to do business. Remember: People do business with people they like.

Power Behind the Throne

As an example of a savvy, versatile woman who gets what she wants, let me tell you the story of my speaking client Belinda Thomas-Parker (name changed by request). She is also one of the most successful trainers I have ever met. In large part, both are due to her unremitting focused tenacity. Belinda is a perfect example of a woman who simply "does what it takes to get the job done," switching from the feminine to the masculine on a moment's notice. Read the following story that she told me when I interviewed her. See if you can pick up where she switched her strategy.

"I am better at negotiation with women than men," Belinda said. "I think it comes from all the male figures from my childhood that I didn't deal with. I went to an all girls' school. I was fired from my first job by a man. It's good for me that I deal with a lot of women in my business. You see some strange stuff when you deal with women all day long in a negotiation situation.

"A lot of people think they can get what they want by being upset or just addressing their own needs. A few months ago, I approached a mid-sized professional association about doing a program at their upcoming annual conference. I sent them some information and they agreed to take a meeting with me because I would be in their town that month anyway on personal matters.

"I arrived at the meeting planner's office. Barbara is in charge of hiring all the trainers each year for the association, and Jane is in charge of the whole annual conference. I knew from other speakers that these two are pretty tough to deal with, so I was already on edge. But once you get in and they like you (and you do a good job), it's a lot of business each year. I really wanted it.

"I was gracious to the secretary. I was on time and prepared. I waited nearly 20 minutes for them to both arrive so the meeting could start, which put me off a little bit. When I met them, I showed them the testimonials from other companies I'd worked for, and explained the outline of my program. I wouldn't have gotten even this far if I hadn't already warmed up Barbara by phone, but it was still a bit nerve-wracking.

"Honestly, they didn't give me much respect. Jane was acting like she just didn't have time to deal with me at all. She was tapping her foot and not paying attention, as if she was too important to be sitting there. It seemed rather immature and certainly impolite. Barbara was obviously second in command to Jane, so I could see all her posturing on the phone didn't mean much after all.

"After 20 minutes of waiting for them, being treated like I was in the way, and answering Jane's rather brisk questions, I knew that everything I was going to do for them wouldn't work anyway. I stood up and started to pack up my demo video and brochures.

"Jane asked me, 'What are you doing?'

"I said, 'I've really tried to create a positive business relationship with you these last few months. I know my training work has helped similar companies, and I came here today because I know it would help you, too. But it appears to me that you are just too busy for this meeting, and so I believe it would be best if I left and you could get on with whatever is next on your to-do list. I regret imposing on you both.' I know that if you are ultra-polite and nice, they can't blame you for anything. Even if they get upset, you will leave and not burn your bridges.

"They sat and looked at one another for a second or two. My heart was beating so loud I couldn't breathe. I was just about to put the last thing in my satchel and Jane suddenly says, 'I like your style. We want to hire you for both of these trainings.' She asked Barbara to do the paperwork, shook my hand, and walked out. I didn't see her again until September, when she complimented me after one of my presentations at the conference. I made $5,500 for standing my own ground! Better yet, Barbara is planning to use me for two more special events next year!"

Obviously, Belinda picked up the more masculine side of her personality when she refused to sit there and be treated like she was annoying Jane and Barbara. By taking command of the situation, she created a powerful change in force and got her desired result.

I've observed myself that some personalities seem to thrive on conflict. I think businesspeople who are in tough jobs sometimes seem to realize they are jerking your chain and you've had it. It's similar to how children test adults, trying to see how far they can push before you snap. In these situations, trust your instincts and take a stand for yourself.

The Auction/Scarcity Model

If you knew that your local Nordstrom was going to have an 80-percent-off sale on every item in the store for the first 200 customers who visit between 3 a.m. and 4 a.m. on Tuesday, would you be there? I'll guess yes. Why? Because a sale is an artificial "event" that generates attention. In this case, the idea of 80 percent off engenders massive interest among the Nordstrom shoppers—mostly women like us who prefer quality clothing at a fair price.

It would easily be worth it to 200 women to be there at 3 a.m. Shopping or sleeping, shopping or sleeping? It's not that hard a choice when we're talking about 80 percent off! At 2 a.m., the parking lot would probably be littered with sleeping bags and women sleeping in their cars, like kids at a rock concert.

But have you ever seen a regular 10- to-20-percent-off sale during regular store hours? Of course you have. And isn't there a quiet frenzy as women rush into the aisles seeking some precious garment that will make them lose 20 years or 20 pounds? We're talking a measly dollar off a $10 item. And some people will still get as excited about it as if it were 80 percent off.

It's human nature.

And in this truth, we have a major negotiation benefit for you. It's called, "Discounting" or "Limited Time Offer." The health club for which I worked offered you a great deal *if* you signed up on your first visit to the club. A lot of people signed up. Maybe a few came back and heard the exact same pitch a week later. Who knows?

When I bought a car a few years ago, the salesman said, "I can give it to you for this price right now, if you take it today. My regular manager won't be in the rest of the week, and he is a lot tougher." I believed him because I wanted to sign the deal, not because I really believed him. I took the car.

Creating "urgency" in negotiation is always a good idea. In August and September, the publishing industry creates a natural urgency for writers who are looking to be trained by my company to create and sell their books. This is because I can honestly say that from January through March, 50 to 60 percent of all the books sold all year are sold. The training takes at least three months. Counting back (and excusing Christmas), you'd better sign up in August or September to make the "buying frenzy" that happens in the first quarter.

If you were negotiating to install a heating system in someone's home in July, you don't have much leverage. But if you point out that if they sign up today, they not only get a discount but that you can't install it until mid-August, when maybe it starts to be cool in the evenings, you have gotten a little leverage.

In publishing when more than one publishing house wants a particular book, we create an "auction"—that is, a date I choose on which all offers for the book must be delivered. It's a largely arbitrary date, but it helps the publishers refer to the project with urgency, and it also drastically increases the amount of money the author will make on the project. Further, it helps everyone view the project correctly: as a very valuable, desirable, limited quantity product. In fact, there's only one.

That's why sales pitches often say, "Just two left!" or "Accepting offers until Wednesday." You can use some of these same factors in your negotiation. While I strongly object to lying in a business situation, it is certainly in your best interest to get more than one company interested in whatever you are offering if it isn't a commodity.

Sandy Levin, a dotcom genius, had built a site that was attracting a huge number of women in their 40s and 50s through her own continual, enormous personal efforts. Another Internet-based company wanted "in" on access to Sandy's customer list. The negotiations dragged on. The second company was smaller, and promised a piece of the future in return for a link to Sandy's goods present day. It wasn't in her favor.

Here's what she had to say.

"They were dragging their feet. They couldn't grow their company without my list or a ton of effort, and I actually thought they had a good plan, but I needed to see their money up front. They were trying to make this deal without giving any cash to me at all. They had a big fat infusion of venture capital, so I knew they had it. Not paying me anything, well, that just wasn't going to work.

"I did a little research and discovered they were afraid of their big competitor, and were trying to catch up to them, which is partly why they wanted my list access. Suddenly, I had some leverage.

"I went to the bigger company, who considered me a small fish by comparison. The Internet world was like that then. It was the little fish getting eaten by a bigger, and those getting eaten by a still bigger, and so on. So I went to them and opened negotiations. Well, actually, I just called them and talked to someone for a half hour or so. They didn't really get excited, but the door was open if I wanted to pursue it.

"I called the smaller company and said, 'Hey, just wanted you to know I've got some other interest, so no hard feelings if you guys can't come up with a deal for me that works. Thanks for your interest.' I actually left that on the voice mail! Can you believe it?

"An hour later, they offered me close to $100,000 for my list, and a percentage of revenues from the hits that converted. That was so cool. I couldn't have done it if I hadn't gotten the bigger company involved. And, I walked out with $98,500 in my pocket. It made the down payment on my house because I put in a little effort to create some heat."

In Summary

Taking decisive, powerful, massive action stimulates the other party to do the same. The job is to create a sense of urgency, and make clear your desire to conclude the deal in a timely manner.

CHAPTER 23

Taking It Personally

> "I think we have a weakness as women. We are
> more sensitive. It's easy to take disagreement in a
> negotiation personally. It's an important skill or
> awareness, that we can take it all too personally.
> It's isn't about 'me' it's about the situation
> being discussed."
> —Jeanne Coughlin, author,
> *The Rise of Female Entrepreneurs*

Have you ever felt like people were talking about you behind your back? It's probably a leftover fear from middle school, when, chances are, they were. But as adults, we sometimes forget that most other people are so busy, so preoccupied, so distracted that they aren't thinking about you and your needs most of the time.

Jeanne Coughlin, whom we met in Chapter 10, has enlightened opinions about most women's tendency to take it personally. Her insights help us see more clearly how we might contribute to our own negotiation challenges:

"I think that women are better at negotiation because we have higher emotional intelligence," Jeanne says. "The more we learn about the Emotional Intelligence Model, the more it helps us understand ourselves. The Emotional Intelligence Model (written about by author/researcher Daniel Goleman in *Emotional Intelligence* [Bantom, 1997]), gives us a phraseology that explains why women are more intelligent and 'in the moment' in relationships and negotiations.

"I definitely think many (not all) women generally have higher emotional intelligence. The soft skills are stronger in women than they are in men a lot of the time. The soft skills are empathy, listening, caring about the others' feelings, and being able to communicate them back as part of your message. All these natural skills help women. It's important to use these skills consciously.

"Personally, I negotiate in our family. If we're leasing or buying a new car, or purchasing business equipment or dealing with service providers, I do the negotiation.

"We recently negotiated the lease of a new car. We'd done a lot of research and the salesman said, 'What, are you crazy? You'd have to own this dealership to get the car at that price!'

"I just stood my ground, and guess what? That's the price I got the car for! I thought there was profit built in for the dealer. Part of the salesman's technique was to shame and embarrass you into thinking you were uninformed and foolish. I didn't get angry. I laughed when he said that. My husband's jaw dropped when he heard that. We know our strengths—my husband and I. He's analytical, so he got all the information together. I am more comfortable with conflict. It feels like conflict when someone's attacking you like that."

"It's important not to be intimidated, and if someone plays the card of emotionality, you can stand your ground if you've done your homework."

> It's important not to be intimidated, and if someone plays the card of emotionality, you can stand your ground if you've done your homework.

"I'm a big believer in saying, 'Get out of here!' with a smile on your face." Coughlin says. "You just need to be consistent and stand your ground.

"In order to not take it personally when someone jumps on you, you have to think calmly. How you react depends on what you're negotiating. If I'm nervous, I ask myself, *Is this a life or death issue? Is it really all that critical?*

"If someone's attacking me or taking a hostile approach, I ask myself how much of this will matter a month or a week from now. It relieves the sting of being personally attacked. When people react hostility or get personal, it says more about them than it does about you.

"At those times, I need to keep centered, not let them pull me in. I need to rely on my strengths. I have seen women lose a negotiation because of the sensitivity they've shown: the cracking voice and the getting emotional, those are the big things. I like laughing, because it proves you're in control. And it's a lot better than being upset.

"Either anger or crying are both wrong extremes. Competent self assurance is the right balance. Always stay in the middle.

"Maybe from experience what I have learned is that at the end of the day if they think I'm not bright, it's not too bad. They're only going to be surprised when they find I am bright. It's part of not being afraid, of not being intimidated into not saying anything. It's part of confidence.

"Confidence in negotiation means knowing that strength is in following their gut and following what comes naturally." she says. *(I want to remind you that confidence also means keeping centered and calm during the negotiation, so you can be as objective as possible as it progresses.)*

Coughlin continues: "There's never anything wrong with taking a break to think things through. Men do this naturally when they are feeling angry with one another in a relationship. We can match their example. It's perfectly acceptable to say, 'I need to get some perspective on this' or 'I need to check in with my research on this before I can answer you. Why don't we reschedule for next week?'"

By stepping back from the emotionality of a negotiation, you save yourself the indignity of crying in a business situation, saying something you'll regret to someone you love, or agreeing to something you don't really want just to "make things better."

I'm Sorry Syndrome

You probably have a girlfriend who apologizes for everything. You're late for your lunch date with her, you blame traffic, and she apologizes!

An interior designer I know apologized for the work of her subcontractors, even before the customer determined whether or not they liked the work. Her trained eye sees flaws the average homeowner would never notice.

Sorry is a catchall word women bandy around to mean, "I empathize with what happened to you" or "I regret you had that experience." It's not likely that she's taking responsibility for the traffic, or the wallpaper hangers who did a job all but perfect to the naked eye.

The problem is the meaning of the word, sorry. Women get mad that many men won't apologize, won't say they are sorry. Sorry puts you in the underdog position, makes you look weak. If you are someone who uses sorry indiscriminately, start discriminating!

If you are 10 minutes late to a negotiation (which of course you shouldn't ever be), the best way to handle it is briefly. Phyllis Davis, founder of ABETA and author of *E2: The Power of Ethics and Etiquette in Business* (Entrepreneur Media Inc., 2003), says the best way to handle a business faux pas is to briefly and simply acknowledge it and then never mention it again.

For example:

"I apologize for being a bit late. Bad accident on the 405. Shall we get to business, then?"

"I got so excited about what our companies can do, I forgot myself, Mr. Bennis. I apologize for knocking over your water glass."

Don't be sorry, instead apologize.

Never Let 'Em See You Cry

Business negotiations are technically between one impersonal company and another impersonal company. There's no room for tears any more than there is room for anger.

If your termite exterminator came by and began sobbing for the lives of the poor little bugs, would you let him do the job?

If your secretary had tears spring to her eyes every time you pointed out a mistake on her paperwork, how long would you keep her?

Crying around people makes them feel awkward. They don't know what to do. They may want to help, or simply run away and not deal with you. Tears are an automatic response to stress in some women. A negotiation starts going wrong, someone says something personal, and it's easy to melt into tears.

You must *never* do this. Cry at home, cry in car on the way back to the office, but never cry in a business situation, with the singular exception of hearing about the serious injury or death of a close colleague or someone in their immediate family.

Men expect women to cry in business, and the more we show them our healthy, natural reaction to circumstances, the more we "prove" in the minds of certain types of men that we are not qualified for the roles we are playing in "their" business world. This is even truer in the more "manly" industries of manufacturing, athletics, anything to do with machines or engines, and traditional blue-collar jobs.

Don't give people the satisfaction of seeing they hurt or frustrated you. If you can't control the onset of tears, excuse yourself to the restroom, get it over with, fix your makeup, and return with your tough outer shell on. Right or wrong, it's got to be done. This applies to whether you are dealing with another woman or with a man.

Katrina's Tears

A while back, I hired another associate agent to work with me. She had all the right credentials: a degree in literature from an upper crust school, a sales background, a charming phone manner, and a passion for reading. Katrina was a needle in the haystack. If she performed well, she could expect a six-figure commission-based income in the first year of working with me. We were both ecstatic.

Within days, my other employees didn't like her. I couldn't figure it out. This tall, pretty, vivacious blond was the epitome of charming when she was around me. I asked my administrative assistant why no one else liked her but me. She smiled and shrugged. I could tell she knew but was trying to be polite and fair.

Two days later, my administrative assistant came to me nearly in tears. She sat down and said, "I don't want to tell you this. It's been bothering me since we talked a few days ago. But Katrina doesn't work when you are not here, or when your office door is closed. She just calls her friends and a caterer and other people related to some big party she's planning. Her boyfriend calls a half dozen times a day. She's ripping you off, Wendy."

I couldn't believe it! Katrina, this sweet, smart young woman? I was incredulous. Could my administrative assistant just be jealous? So within an hour, I left the office. I walked around the parking lot and came back in, ostensibly to retrieve something I'd forgotten. I stood three feet from Katrina's desk. Sure enough, she was discussing food selection for a party! I was shocked.

I called her into my office. We had a stern conversation, with her doing most of the listening. She cried. I felt sorry for her, and a little unnerved by her tears. She swore to improve, to tell her live-in boyfriend not to call her at work, and so on. I relented and let her keep her job.

I really did leave for an appointment. My administrative assistant was on lookout. When I walked back in the next morning, she reported that Katrina's promise already hadn't been kept. I was standing in the middle of the office when the phone rang. It was Katrina's boyfriend. After they chatted happily for a few moments, I called her into my office again. She said, "I wrote it down in my Day-Timer to remember to tell him tonight not to call me any more, I promise. I'm so sorry!" More tears.

I said, "Show me your Day-Timer, then."

Katrina blanched. She began mumbling about that page being missing, or perhaps she'd forgotten the whole Day-Timer. It was open on her desk. We walked to it. There was nothing on the page. All the tears in the world couldn't save Katrina now.

A few months later, another employee saw her in a restaurant in town. She'd become a waitress.

Screaming, Anger, and Cussing

The man you are negotiating with is being a big, fat %^&# and you'd love to let him know. Don't. He's using every curse word in the book, and you'd like to trump him with a few of your own. Don't.

Just like your mother always said, don't stoop down to their level. Mom was right. You really are "better than that." Men can get away with keeping their businesses intact and still cuss out everyone within earshot, but a woman cannot. In a negotiation, your job is to play it cool, stay cool, calm, and collected, and to be sure everyone is treated with dignity—including you. If someone is using abusive or rude language in your presence, you are completely entitled to walk out or hang up.

A man I knew in business uses expletives in every other sentence. He runs a food distribution company, and has become successful enough (and old enough) to be entitled to be a jerk, in his own opinion. Strangely, I believe he thinks his rudeness and short temper are what made him successful! He's in his 80s now. He's definitely part of a dying breed.

The double standard certainly exists for women. No matter what the male says, the woman must never use similar language without knowing it may risk the deal. Don't lose your tongue or your temper if you want to keep the negotiation moving forward.

In Summary

Business and negotiation are not venues for emotionality. Whether one is negotiating with a boss, a customer, or a loved one, tears, rage, and emotional outbursts do not belong in successful negotiations, and can often undermine them.

CHAPTER 24

Learning "Politician Speak"

"I did not have sex with Monica Lewinsky."
—Former President Bill Clinton, shortly before he
defined oral sex as not being real sex

Medicare and Medicaid services have nominated a man named Dr. Mark McClellan the position of administrator. In order to secure the nomination, it appears that Dr. McClellan had to sit before the "Prescription Drug Committee," a group of very old politicians who are interested in benefits for seniors.

While watching C-Span is typically soporific for me, I was fascinated by the negotiation techniques used by both Dr. McClellan and his adversary of the moment, Senator Frank Lautenberg (D-New Jersey).

Dr. McClellan had just been asked quite clearly about his position on importing drugs from Canada for Medicare patients. He basically said, "At this time, the current legislation is yet unclear as to the advantages...." Blah, blah, blah. Basically, he gave no answer.

Then it was Sen. Lautenberg's turn to grill Dr. McClellan. With a thinly veiled razor blade of compliments hidden below his silk handkerchief of intention, the senator plied Dr. McClellan with overt compliments. His performance was worthy of the most notorious maneuverings of the French court before the storming of the Bastille and the Revolution. One half expected him to don a powdered wig and pull a rapier from his scabbard.

He complimented McClellan's artful use of language, and then said, "Now, my hearing is just fine. But I've been listening to you and I can't understand yet…" what McClellan's position was on the drug importation issue.

McClellan apologized graciously to the old gentleman, and then threw up a bunch of acronyms that probably mean something to the people in the room, citing their inconclusive research as being the vital key to his decision, should he become the administrator.

Lautenberg made comments on how learned and wise McClellan is, "despite his youth," which he apparently envies.

Lautenberg pulled a sheaf of papers out and read a report done in 2000, reporting on the savings a learned expert said were possible— some $35 billion per year if that man's suggestions were immediately implemented. Like a hawk, Lautenberg's thinly veiled eyes observed the proceeding as if he were perched on the flagpole above the room. He asked McClellan how it was that he (McClellan) had estimated the savings to the American public would be only $30 billion during the next 10 years.

McClellan had an answer. But in the entire exchange, it was nearly impossible to see which one was excelling. They were like two Sumo wrestlers circling the mat, neither engaging in anything but the most pleasant and gentlemanly conversation.

Each man had his professional reputation and his income at stake. If the Senator failed to protect the rights of seniors in his state, surely he would lose their vote. If McClellan didn't win the nomination, probably he would not only be embarrassed but he would lose what was probably a significant income from the job. With so much at stake, it was interesting to see them "dance" around the issue, each appearing to answer on the surface, but not directly answer the question.

We are accustomed to this behavior from our politicians. But did you know that when companies such as mine train people to appear for the media, we teach them to do the same thing?

Remember when Prince Charles admitted his affair with Camilla Parker-Bowles on national U.K. television? Someone hadn't trained him properly, or he forgot his training for a moment.

Honesty is the best policy, except when saying too much will get you in more trouble than it's worth. Then it's best to say *less*.

In a negotiation with particularly skilled negotiators, the "tough guys," you will sometimes run into people who flatter you, compliment you, and then go for the jugular, tripping you up on what you've just said, misunderstanding or distorting your words. It's like watching Perry Mason—except it's your life!

The Lady's Guide to Creating a Poker Face

Negotiation can be a little bit like theater. You are in a starring role. Your antagonist is the person with whom you are negotiating, and you are the suave, charming, beautiful protagonist.

If you are negotiating for something you *love* and can scarcely imagine living without, like the perfect sofa or a car that's in the color you dream about, your role is to *act as if you don't care*. You already know when you walk into a house that's for sale, you're supposed to *not* let the Realtor know you've fallen in love the second you crossed the threshold. This is true of all negotiations.

You are in the strongest position in negotiation when you *really don't care*. You are in the weakest position when you *must* make it happen.

In between the two positions are caring and showing it. Your goal is to learn to care and *not* show it. You want to be calm, pleasant, professional, impassive, and, above all, prepared to walk.

> You have the greatest power only when you are prepared to walk away from the deal if fair terms cannot be met.

We often wear the enthusiasm and desire we have for something on our sleeves, especially as women. We're socialized to respond. We say, "Mmm-hmmm" to our child as we're cooking dinner, and "How interesting!" to our spouse at the same time. We listen to our girlfriends tell us their woes with empathy. We say, "Oh, I can't believe it!"

and "You poor thing!" and a thousand other murmurings. We are excited when we are excited, sad when we are sad, scared when we are scared.

Men don't do it that way. "Big boys don't cry" and all that. In negotiation, men don't get emotional, unless it's to get angry, and when that happens, the angry guy loses.

Our goal is to learn to stay cool, calm, and collected even in the heat of the moment.

The following are some tips on how to do that:

Tip for Staying Cool, Calm, and Collected

1. Breathe a few deep breaths before you walk into the meeting.

2. Visualize it all turning out just perfectly, everyone smiling at the end.

3. Wear clothes with which you don't have to fuss. No skirts that ride up, no blouses that peek, no sloppy clothes, no brand-new shoes. You want to be totally focused, look professional, look good, feel good.

4. Practice a few "stock phrases" in advance, so you have them on "automatic" in case you start to get emotional. Try, "I'll give that some thought," or "I can see that is your point of view," or perhaps, "I'll have to consider that." One of my favorites is, "I hadn't thought of that."

5. Be prepared to walk.

The final tip of number 4, "I hadn't thought of that," is my favorite defense against macho-style salesmen who are trying to find my hot buttons. In sales terminology, *hot buttons* are the emotional triggers that make people—mostly females—buy. You've heard them when the clerk in the dress store not only tells you how flattering the dress is, but enlists another employee to agree with her. (Sorry, girls. It's a parlor trick. It may not be true.)

Linda Allen, single mother and sales professional, tells this story: "When I bought my most recent car, a red Jaguar, I was buying it because Lexus had told me they couldn't get me a car in the shade of black cherry pearl for at least six months, because they were back-ordered. I had been loyal to Lexus until then. So I drove two blocks to the Jaguar dealer. I had seen the same color on a car in the front of the lot. I knew I wanted the car. I knew I wanted the car for the dumbest of all possible reasons. The prices between the cars were similar. The features were similar. I wanted that color, and that was that.

"The older sales guy said, 'What makes you want a Jaguar?' What a great sales question! It assumes I want a Jaguar. I didn't particularly care about the make, so it was easy for me to say, 'I don't know yet if I want a Jaguar, frankly.' I said.

"He said, 'Okay, well, let's look around and see if we can't find something you like.' I let him show me three other cars before we got to the one I wanted. I appeared apathetic about all four of them, although I test drove two. I was feeling proud of myself. 'You like the red one best, don't you?' I was a little shocked that he'd picked that up.

"I caught myself and said, 'I hadn't thought of that.'

"Straight out of a sales training manual, he said, 'So what are you looking for in a car?' I went on about Lexus and how it was superior to any other car I'd ever owned. While I was doing this, I was digging my own pit. I knew it. He knew it. Why didn't I shut up?

"All he had to do was ask, 'So why are you here?' He did. I reverted to my stock phrases. 'You know, I had to see what else is out there. You know, check the competition just in case.'

"I felt myself panicking inside. Somehow, it's easier for me to negotiate for business than for personal things. I wondered how he knew I wanted the red one. I had been careful not to tell him how much I wanted it.

"That night, I left my old car there and drove off with the red one. The deal was fair, but I suspect I could have done better if I'd stayed even less attached to the car, and if I'd really been prepared to walk away."

You Gotta Know When to Hold 'Em, Know When to Fold 'Em

Developing a "poker face"—the appearance of nonchalance—and matching it with an attitude of nonchalance are critical skills in negotiation.

The most important advantage you can have is to *be prepared to walk.* By realizing that you have other options to almost any deal, you give yourself the power to walk away from the table. That removes your emotional attachment to the deal. There's another car, another house, another job, another guy, even another husband down the road.

A business mentor once told me that the greatest advantage of being an entrepreneur is that you don't have to work with people you don't like. When a customer who is going to be needy comes to the agency for help, I simply pass. I am prepared to walk. We've turned away two celebrity memoirs because the "headache factor" was too much, despite the commission we would have earned. A few times, I have used the cancel clause in the contract when the author became pushy, rude, or demanding toward my staff or me.

A few weeks ago, a man came in seeking representation of his book about building powerful networking relationships. I would not have taken his call, but he was recommended by an esteemed peer.

He began at once. "Wendy, how are you?" Pause.

I have never spoken to this man before. I say the standard, "Fine."

He said, "Really? Are you really fine?"

Slightly annoyed, I said, "Yes. Now can you please tell me why you are calling?"

"I've got a book that will change your life, Wendy," he said. "It will teach you things you never even dreamed were possible about networking. Are you married? Do you have kids?"

I was fully annoyed, but still being polite. "I have a daughter," I replied.

He launches into how I can use it to help her make more friends at school. I'm ready to hang up. I interrupted him. "What are your credentials for writing this book?"

I always ask that question, because the answer determines how much I can sell the book for, and if I can sell it.

He blathers on about how he had, "all the credentials in the world," and I would quickly find that out when he Fed Ex'd me his project for early delivery tomorrow. He asked if he could call me in the afternoon for my response.

I told him no, he could send it any method he pleased and I would read it on my own schedule, in order, as I do everything else.

He reminded me that a colleague sent him to me, and asked if he shouldn't get priority treatment.

I firmly agree to read it as soon as I could, and hung up. You can guess what happened. He called the next afternoon, told my assistant it was a "personal call" and was put through. I was livid. I told him I would not be representing him or his book, and that we would return it to him. (Remember, it's about creating *successful* business relationships!)

We sent it back. He sent me a rude, insulting letter accusing me of being unprofessional by rejecting him without actually reading the manuscript, and of being insensitive and dishonest because I did not read his material the afternoon "I promised." He alerted me that he was copying our mutual acquaintance with the e-mail so he could see what sort of person I was "after all."

If, next year, I discover someone else sold his book, or if I discover he makes the *New York Times* best-seller list, I will have a half pang of regret that I couldn't tolerate his surly attitude. But I was prepared to walk. I had all the power. His anger and misdirected rage cost him at least my support. Most agents would have passed on him, except for the new ones who have no choice but to work with difficult clients while they establish themselves. Been there, done that.

This ability to walk comes in handy in parenting. If you say, "If you don't eat your dinner, you won't get dessert" you have to be prepared to enforce your decision—the equivalent of walking on the deal. The child, of course, will be angry and the connection will be broken momentarily. But are you prepared to walk?

Perhaps you want a particular sofa from a large retail establishment. It's beautiful and it goes perfectly with your décor, but you are a smart negotiator. You do not show your enthusiasm for it to the salespeople. You smile a half smile and say, "What can you sell this to me for?"

If you have a shopping partner with you, you can say aloud, "Well, Chris, I don't know. I like it but it's a little too expensive. You know that one we saw yesterday would maybe be a better deal." The salesperson hungry to make a deal will think, "price objection" and speak up within minutes, perhaps with some fanfare of talking to the manager, with the best counter offer he or she can make. If you stick to your guns, there's probably a better deal just below that "deal." It is those who can hold out the longest, without appearing to want the deal to be done, who will win.

If you're shopping alone, you ask a lot of qualifying questions. These are called "buying signals" in sales training. The salesperson is trained to start counting how they'll spend their commission when you start to ask "buying questions." These are: When can it be delivered? How much does it cost? What are your terms? Are you flexible on the price? Any question that identifies you as having a specific interest in that specific item is a "buying signal." (For a detailed list, refer to Chapter 10.)

Use it to your advantage. Start by asking buying questions about something you have little to no intention of buying. "This orange Formica dinette set, how much is it? Does it come with these chairs? Do you deliver on Saturdays? Do these ever go on sale?"

Find out how hungry the salesperson is by watching him jump on your words when you are talking about something you not only can but will walk away from.

Move over to the item in which you are interested. Ask your buying questions with the exact same tone of voice as you used when you really were prepared to walk. The salesperson is either thinking, *Gosh! They're going to buy the whole store!* (if they are naïve). Or, *This person can't make up their mind between a recliner and a dinette set. I'll play it low key since this is a looker, not a buyer.* (The latter gives you a chance to lead the conversation into the general state of sales in the store, maybe even how much longer that salesperson intends to stay there, how many of these move out in a month, and so on). Or even, *Great! They are going to buy the chair and I make more commission on this anyway.*

You want to keep your advantage by asking questions in a non-committal way. The longer you keep them guessing about the sale, the longer you have to gain information on the spot. It's sort of like the game of "blink" that we played as kids. You stare into the other person's eyes and the loser is the first one to blink. Remember, the longer it's apparent you can walk, the more power you have.

It's not cruel, it's business.

Just as Sen. Lautenberg did, the best thing you can do is be overly prepared. By having all your "ducks in a row" you can say what you mean and nothing more.

This means you need to be prepared for what salespeople call "overcoming objections." If you are not prepared, you run the risk of talking yourself into a corner, making promises you and your company can't keep, or simply embarrassing yourself.

In Summary

"Least said, soonest mended" is true some of the time. You don't have to tell someone all your flaws on the first date, but you also cannot ever lie.

CHAPTER 25

Overcoming Objections

"The harder the conflict, the more glorious the triumph. What we obtain too cheap, we esteem too lightly; it is dearness only that gives everything its value. I love the man that can smile in trouble, that can gather strength from distress and grow brave by reflection. 'Tis the business of little minds to shrink; but he whose heart is firm, and whose conscience approves his conduct, will pursue his principles unto death."
—Thomas Paine, patriot, writer

Many times in a negotiation we're going to be stymied. We've run headlong into the other person's fears, or they've ensnared us in their clever language.

The administrative assistant worries that if she buys toner from your company, it may not be as good as that of their previous supplier, even though it will save money.

Dr. McClellan might have panicked and started yelling at the crafty old senator.

The wife is concerned that if she makes this large a purchase without telling her husband, there could be problems at home.

The other party isn't sure they trust you yet, or that the deal is good for them, so they raise a whole list of concerns. Sales books and sales teachers tell you that if objections occur, it's because you haven't taught the other party enough yet to overcome their fears. The negotiation is complete when both parties believe the transaction is worth the exchange of what one values for what the other values, for example money for knowledge.

It's also a good sign. People with objections are simply saying, "I'm not quite sold yet. Please help me make up my mind."

The Ultimate Sales Perspective
Yes means money,
maybe means yes,
And no means maybe.

The more you know about yourself, your product, the process of negotiation, and the other party before you walk into the negotiation, the more likely you are to succeed. You will want to research in advance the likeliest objections, and be prepared to overcome them. That's a factor of listening (old fashioned research—perhaps even to the point of sleuthing).

Jan Austin, International Coach Federation leader and renowned business coach, agreed to be interviewed. She told me:

"I have learned the most important part of a negotiation is much more clearly listening to what the prospect wants to buy. I know what I want, but then I have to listen carefully to what they say. It's much harder to hear what they really *need* than listen to them say what they really *want*. I think that one of the big mistakes women make is not listening for what other people need. On top of that, a lot of women don't state what they want. They hint, they hope. We need to get clear, ask clear questions, and listen for clear answers.

"In my own career, I notice that some people think they don't need to work with a coach. They don't see the value in having someone clear away the clutter that is blocking them from their goals. Sometimes I'm able to successfully negotiate with them. I say, 'I understand you have some reservations and you need to be sure about this, so let's have two or three sessions and then we'll see where we go from there.' Nine times out of 10, making that offer will sell them.

"One of the things people sometimes need is to try before they buy. It gives people first-hand experience, so whatever reservations they have, I overcome those reservations. It's easy for me to offer that. It costs me nothing but time.

"With corporate clients who are eager, I will suggest they start with the six-months package and I tell them it is renewable. Six months is completely easy for most people. 'Try before you buy, make a smaller commitment before you make the bigger one.' Knowing what to offer comes from listening for what they really need." Jan concluded.

So how do you get prepared to negotiate and overcome objections? If you've done your preparation, you understand where the other side is coming from and you know what's likely to bother them. A salesperson hears the same objections to their product or service over and over again. The similarity of the objections leads her to create a stock phrase or plan for overcoming that objection before it even occurs.

You can apply this technique to your negotiations, whether they are unique one-time-only negotiations, interpersonal negotiations, or something you negotiate for or about on a regular basis.

Because you will have already determined what you ideally want, and planned to get it, and because you have probably already thought through how you are going to present the negotiation yourself, and the logical conclusion to the customer, you need to know how to bullet-proof your negotiation.

All things being equal, the easiest way to prepare to overcome objections is to know what they are likely to be in advance.

Put yourself in the other person's high heels:

- Will she want to be reassured your company will fulfill its promises on time?
- Does she seem likely to be most concerned that she'll look good to her boss for choosing to work with you?
- Is she shopping primarily price?
- What are her "hot buttons"—the things that are most important to her?

You will learn a lot of this by listening to the other person speak, but ideally, you will have asked questions and gotten these answers before the actual negotiation takes place. Only then will you have a clear path to prepare to overcome these objections.

When I am negotiating with someone, I will usually do so by telephone. It's the nature of my industry. Often, I will say, "If I can provide you with the terms you just asked for, will you be ready to sign a contract?"

The other party will either give me more objections at this point, or they will say, "Yes." At that point, it's up to me to find ways to meet the terms if I can.

By asking in advance, I am "thrashing the bunnies out of the bushes"—I'm coming within a hair's breadth of closing the negotiation in everyone's favor.

Once I know what the other party is concerned about, I brainstorm on how I can make it work:

- Does she object to my price? Can I offer a discount? How much? Under what conditions? Will I give her a discount only if she refers six of her friends to me?

- How about a payment plan or a performance percentage to compensate for income not made on the front end?

- Can I prove the value of the price I am asking by showing how other people earned back three to nine times what they paid for the same material—within a few weeks or months? Can I show her testimonials from them?

- Can I connect her by e-mail or phone to my happy customers?

- What's my real hard cost of goods—can I lower the price if that's what it will take?

- Is she worried about how she'll appear to her boss for choosing to work with us?

- Can I offer her a letter commending her on her choice?

- Can I guarantee the service we're offering?

- Can I offer to send a letter to her boss complimenting him on employing such a wise negotiator?

- Can I provide her with documentation to take to her boss to prove we excel at serving these sorts of customers?

- ❧ Can I invite myself to show up on her site and meet her boss along with her?
- ❧ Is she concerned I won't deliver the service in a timely manner?
- ❧ Can I provide her with a chart that shows precisely when each item will be met?
- ❧ Can I provide a penalty to myself for not meeting those deadlines—a refund to her perhaps, or an extra month of service?
- ❧ What's my record of on-time delivery of the service?
- ❧ Would she have been more comfortable if I gave myself two months to meet the goal, instead of three weeks?
- ❧ How good is my guarantee?

Write out the answers to objections you have heard, expect to hear what they would ask in the situation. Be clear, be succinct in your responses, and memorize them so that you can answer confidently when you are in the "heat of it."

In Summary

Being ready to overcome objections by thinking through what could go wrong before it does is a critical success strategy in all negotiations.

CHAPTER 26

Country, Mom, and Apple Pie

"If you want to make an apple pie from scratch,
you must first create the universe."
—Carl Sagan, author, scientist

You're having a holiday party Saturday. You've got the menu planned in your head. It's going to be nice. But your friend calls you Thursday and asks you to let her Aunt Marla come over, too. She's in town for the holiday and your friend doesn't want to leave her alone. Of course you say yes, it's no trouble at all.

What do you do now? You squish everyone in a little bit around your table. Instead of six, it will seat seven. You put on an extra potato, or steam a few more spears of asparagus.

Saturday evening, everyone has a terrific time. Your Aunt Betty and your friend's aunt really hit it off. The two even plan on keeping in touch. Aunt Marla was delightful company. Later, she even pulls you aside to tell you what a lovely holiday she's had.

No bother, right? It all turned out fine.

Just like you were able to accommodate Aunt Marla at dinner, you are able to do the same in a negotiation. You want a bigger piece of the pie? Simply learn to make a bigger pie!

It's not difficult, no more trouble than having an extra person over for dinner.

When you stop thinking of the world as finite, your life and your actions as restricted, and you think of yourself as the powerful woman you are, you will see that all around you are the ingredients you need to create a bigger pie.

Practically speaking, how does that work?

Pies That Float

Having listened to what the other party *really* wants, we can negotiate so that all our needs get met. It reminds me of a prosperous professional speaker I know. His consulting help on how a yacht retailer could increase sales was sorely needed. The company had almost no sales, and no solutions. Of course, they also had no money. But they did have inventory. My friend, a master at "bigger pie" thinking, volunteered to consult the company—in return for a free yacht! The $60,000 yacht was delivered to the lake near his home in upstate New York. But he took it a step further. He found a couple in his country club who also wanted a yacht, but couldn't afford the $60,000. He sold them half interest in his new boat. Not only did the yacht maker benefit by greatly increased sales, but the friends at the country club got half-use of a brand-new boat, and my friend was in possession of a beautiful new yacht, and $30,000 up on the deal—about what his consulting would have cost in the first place!

> "A mother is a person who when seeing there
> are only four pieces of pie for five people,
> promptly announces she never did care for pie."
> —Tenneva Jordan

Big Books, Bigger Pie

Oftentimes a publisher will be nervous about how successful a new book will be, no matter how confident I am in the author. To buffer all our fears, it is customary to negotiate "list bonuses." These mean that should the book hit a best-seller list, typically the *New York Times*, the author will instantly be entitled to a large chunk of cash. Why does this work? Because should the book "hit the list," the publisher will immediately see a huge chunk of cash from the book sales. The publisher is out nothing if it doesn't, it gives the author a chance to prove his or her work on the open market, and it also motivates the author to work hard to make things happen.

Make Your Own Pie

Creativity is a critical component in successful negotiations. The following are a few ways you can create a "bigger pie" in your negotiations:

- ♣ Offer to trade professional services.
- ♣ Offer to refer clients or help market a vendor's business.
- ♣ Trade babysitting or carpooling duties.
- ♣ Offer a performance bonus.
- ♣ Offer commission on quotas exceeded.
- ♣ Share your housekeeper one day a week.
- ♣ Give your spouse a long back massage for his taking your car in for service.
- ♣ Offer two athletic event tickets to the contractor if he finishes by the weekend.
- ♣ Promise your 12-year-old a cell phone if she gets straight As this semester.

> "The fellow who says he'll meet you halfway usually thinks he's standing on the dividing line."
> —Orlando A. Battista, author

Should You Undersell to Get the Deal?

Almost everyone can remember a time they were so desperate to get the deal, they sold themselves short to make it work. I remember spending seven months trying to get a huge corporate client to agree to let us promote 10 seminars for them. The seminar programs would have brought them tens of thousands in business every month. The amount I was asking was quite minor by comparison, but with a percentage of the profit, I believed it would be incredibly lucrative.

The corporation kept hemming and hawing about signing. They needed me to drop my price, they said. So I did. They said they'd "think about it." They asked me to pay for a few more things on their behalf. I agreed. I felt my profits shrinking. I understood it was a new venture for them, but for me it meant adding half a dozen more staff on their behalf. I had people waiting. I was antsy and eager to say the least.

Along the way, I hired a wise old attorney to review the contract changes the company wanted. The gentleman called me and said, "Miss Keller, don't let me tell you how to run your business, but if you do this and anything goes wrong, you are not making enough money off this deal to even cover the cost of administering it. You'd have to be 110-percent certain they'll make $45,000 within the first month for you to even earn your investment back, much less earn a profit. Are you sure you want to do this? I think you're underselling. This is a very big venture."

His words pierced my heart like a poisoned arrow. I realized that along the way, my desire to close the deal had obliterated my common sense about it. I felt so silly when the attorney brought it to my attention. I'd become so focused on the deal being signed, I'd lost sight of the original purpose—to benefit my company and theirs, in that order!

Business coach Jan Austin talks about the tendency to paint ourselves into a corner with "discounting." Lowering your prices or overcommitting to service will make any deal untenable in the long run.

Jan says, "The danger of undervaluing ourselves has consequences. Those consequences are often the sacrifice of our own time and personal value. Discounting attracts a struggling buyer. It's a balancing act. I say instead of discounting, offer something of lesser value. Sometimes, this helps the buyer commit."

In terms of her own business, Jan says, "I sometimes offer one session for free, then they pay slightly discounted rate for the next three months. I focus on the added value I provide. For instance, I offer extremely valuable self-assessments that can make people much more clear about their goals when receiving coaching."

Stores do this when they have "loss leaders," especially around the holidays. Loss leaders are products that most people want. The stores sell them for almost nothing: Lettuce heads at two for a dollar; three six-packs of Coke for $5, right before the Fourth of July; watermelon for 19 cents a pound. You wonder how they make money. They don't on those items. They make money on your fatigue factor. You don't want to go from store to store to store, buying watermelon here, lettuce there, and Coke over there. It's the holidays and you're busy. You'll just shop at the store that seems to have the greatest number of items you want on sale.

This means, while you're there, you'll buy all your other holiday goods at the usual, non-sale price. And if they've got your dollars, the store down the street doesn't. The loss leader got you in, human nature made you spend more money there on other things, and voila! The loss leader is a huge profit center.

Jan Austin continues, "Offering something of lesser cost as an incentive to get the buyer to commit is a good idea. Many people want to commit to you, that's why they are in the negotiation. They want to buy. But what I say is instead of discounting, offer something of lesser value. Ideally, something that costs you next to nothing."

I hear, "lettuce, Coke, and watermelon," when she says that.

Jan teaches us, "We have to look at both sides of the equation. When someone's critical needs are already met, he or she is less price sensitive. If they aren't worried about the rent, you can sell them new furniture, and so on.

"Discounting sets up the cycle for you to attract an unsophisticated, disloyal buyer. They'll go anywhere for a better price. Bargain shoppers keep hopping around. I don't advocate discounting. I think it diminishes our value. We don't want to compete on price. Commodities compete on price and speed of delivery. Brands distinguish based on quality, service, and so on.

"If you want to be a brand that is distinctive and powerful in negotiations, distinguish between discounting and adding value. If I give you something extra, like I do with assessment, you're thinking it is equal to X price. Meanwhile, I didn't discount my time, I did something that cost nothing or very little to give you. That's the best kind of incentive."

In Summary

Creativity is a core ingredient in your success. You must continually look at the situation from every side, especially the other side's side. That way, you can find ways acceptable to you to make the deal acceptable to them.

CHAPTER 27

Speed Bumps

> "While the fates permit, live happily; life speeds on with hurried step, and with winged days the wheel of the headlong year is turned."
> —Seneca (BC 5-65 AD)

My friend Marc Allen and I were on the phone and he was telling me about his principles, as expressed in his life-changing book *The Millionaire Course* (New World Library, 2003). I've known and admired Marc as long as I have been in publishing. He's the author of several valuable books that have shaped my thinking as an entrepreneur, but also he's the publisher of such other great teachers as Eckhardt Tolle, Shakti Gawain, Deepak Chopra, and Jose Stevens, author of *The Power Path* (2002)—a very important book.

Our personality styles are very different. We laugh about it. He believes that success can be created in a relaxed and easy manner. His work appeals to people who want to achieve wealth and success without extreme effort. Me, well, I was born Type A. The very words "relaxed and easy manner" make me cringe! Marc's approach to life's obstacles is to relax into them, meditate on solutions, focus on strength, and visualize success.

For me, that only goes so far. When confronted with an obstacle, my first instinct is to start looking for the keys to my bulldozer.

Negotiation is fraught with speed bumps in most cases. It's part of the deal, part of the territory. Overcoming those speed bumps and getting to a resolution are part of the skills you need as a professional negotiator.

My observation after hundreds and hundreds of contract negotiations is that the most common factor is the human factor.

We've already looked at how to overcome objections (which are often tactics to take you "off the scent" of the deal instead of the real heart of the issue). We've looked also at how to make it a bigger pie, so there's more for everyone. These are critical frames of mind, important distinctions.

But there's often the "heart of the deal" that sometimes gets so covered up you can miss it.

The Heart of the Deal

Classic sales training says if you overcome price, trust, and a few other regular objections, you will create a closed deal. That's sales, not negotiation, and I know it doesn't always work even in sales. Sometimes, there's more than meets the eye. That's when you have to listen and observe with your heart, your feminine intuition.

Business, negotiations, sales, are all about people interacting with people. You may never see the people behind the product, like when you buy a soda from a vending machine. But if the vending machine soda makes you sick, suddenly, you expect to talk to real people—and their lawyers.

The reverse is also true. You can wander through a discount warehouse such as Costco. If you actually find someone who works there whose sole job isn't handing out food treats to try to get you to buy some product, the person will most likely have no idea where something you are looking for is located. I think of this as the "you're on your own" kind of store.

Then across the street from the wholesale warehouse is a Staples. If I dare to even begin to ask a question at Staples, whomever I ask it of will actually take me to the location, wait to answer any new questions, get me help, or whatever I need. It's almost unnerving, but kind of nice. That's the "We're here to help you buy things" kind of store.

Depending on what you like, one is a "relaxed and easy manner" and the other is a "bulldozer." If you prefer "relaxed" then you can certainly know you'll be left alone at Costco, unless you prefer "relaxed" to mean you won't have to think because the Staples person will think for you.

It's all in your perspective. And here's the weird thing about perspective: we all have a different one. Including the people with whom you are trying to negotiate.

Think of the last time you said or heard the phrase, "I'm sure she meant well." We use this excuse for people a lot. It means we understand that they thought what they did was nice. Like the time my daughter, at age 6, "surprised" me by making dinner. She put a dozen eggs and five pounds of sugar in a huge metal bowl, mixed it, put it in the fridge, and told me we were having Jell-O for dinner, her treat! It was cute, and I'm sure she meant well.

Your goal as a female negotiator is to try to find out what is important to the other person. Marketing books abound teaching what's wanted by different segments of the population: speed, personal connection, honesty, a good guarantee, and so forth.

Your grandparents bought Craftsman tools from Sears because they were guaranteed to last forever and you could return them any time if they broke. When's the last time you thought about where to buy the best hammer?

Your child wants an iPod, because she or he can get all the music they want stored in it instead of having to go the music store and "bother" with a CD. Am I the only one who grew up singing to Billy Joel cassettes on a 4-pound battery-operated audiocassette player as big as a phone book—on the seat next to me in the car?

By listening, you will know what the person says they want from the negotiation. But people don't really want "faster delivery" or "a lifetime guarantee" or "money back in return if it breaks." They want more time to do what they want to do—sleep, run, play with their kids. They want not the $10 back, but the time invested that the $10 represents to them, a portion of their hourly wage. Everyone wants this: a quality of life that supports their desires.

Money may not buy happiness,
but it sure makes misery easier to live with.
—Unknown

You seek and find the desire that drives the other person. It's a quality of life we want, not literally the money or convenience that's being offered. Recognize that the other party may be thinking something totally different than you are, something so different you can barely imagine it. Recognize that you are negotiating with people, who have real lives and other things on their minds.

What He Sees When He Looks At You: Men in Negotiation

In her powerful book, *Play Like a Man, Win Like a Woman*, Gail Evans teaches us that men assign to us one of four roles: mother, daughter, wife, or mistress. There is also a fifth in my opinion: sister. The role they cast you in automatically determines how they will relate to you. Ms. Evans is not the first to note that in the workplace, men tend to assign women these roles unconsciously.

It may also be that we assign them father, son, husband, brother, or lover, but my experience and all the research I can find seem to indicate that women are less likely to assign men these roles than the reverse.

Assuming then that, shortly after meeting you, a man has determined in his subconscious which role you will now play, how can you use that assignment to your advantage in a negotiating situation? And how do you know whether the man has a positive or negative association with women in that role in his life? Was his mother a drunken child abuser? Is his wife a shrew who filed for divorce last week and plans to take him for all he's got?

Psychologists refer to a "level-10 response" to a "level-one stimulus." In other words, if someone cuts you off in traffic but no harm was done, and yet you seethe with rage for a half hour, weaving in and out of traffic to try to show the driver your finger, you have overreacted. You've had a level-10 response to a level-one stimulus. Your reaction doesn't fit the "crime."

The fact is, you need to be aware of the possibilities when you deal with other people and when they deal with you. By becoming aware, you get to choose whether or not to "play into" the other parties fears: create scarcity, the "Limited Time Offer" approach, or whether you will play to their higher personal motives, "Doing this will surely get you a raise when your boss learns how much money you saved negotiating with us."

In Summary

Who the other people essentially are is at least as important as the obvious issues. As a smart negotiator, you will prepare and adjust to their personalities to accomplish your goals.

CHAPTER 28

Negotiating
Air

"If you're planning on doing business with someone again, don't be too tough in the negotiations. If you're going to skin a cat,
don't keep it as a house cat."
—Marvin S. Levin, author

Preparation becomes even more of a challenge when what you are negotiating doesn't have a set price. When I sell a book, I know exactly what it will sell for. I always tell the authors up front, "I guarantee this book will sell for between $0 and $2 million in advance."

They laugh. They think I'm joking. But 15 years of selling intangible things like books has taught me that a product is only worth what the market will bear. I live in Malibu now. I sold a 3,500 square foot house in a town I didn't like for a house half that size in a town I do like (for the same price). Transplant the large house here, it would be a celebrity home. Why? Because a product is worth what the market will bear.

If the person with whom you are negotiating is selling you something that has no "actual value"—that is, it's ink on paper or paint on canvas or notes on music sheets—it hasn't got any real value. You may love it, and the next four people may hate it. But if you are willing to pay, say, twice the price the last person was for it, suddenly this intangible product is *worth* twice the price it was before. And it has now grown in value.

This simple, small house I live in has doubled in value in the five years I've owned it. My parents, in Chicago, laugh that I could have two mansions in their town for the same price. And it's true. My house is worth more simply because someone wants to say it is.

When you are researching the value of an intangible, your job is to compare it to the most similar products out there. The advance my publisher paid for this book is far smaller than the advance John Grisham's publisher paid for his last book. Why? The product is worth only and precisely what the market will bear.

But if this book went on to be an international best-seller (which I know from my own experience is not likely), suddenly my next book would be worth 10, 20, 50 times more than my current publisher is paying.

As a person negotiating on behalf of the intangible and trying to convince the other party it has value, you must first determine which factors are important to the other party. If I sell a book to a publisher, I want to know if they want it because of its powerful author, the fact the author can help sell lots of copies, the content of the book itself, and so on.

Take this example from my interview with art dealer/entrepreneur Bonnie Paul:

"I negotiate with corporations on the price of the art they will be acquiring. My customer, or end user, is usually an architect or designer. On the other side, I am negotiating with the artist, gallery, or publisher I represent. I'm the go-between.

"I've got to make sure I take care of both sides. I do this by being fair. I also have learned what it will take to get the work sold. I know what price points I can offer a piece at without overcharging or giving too deep a discount. I learned this through experience.

"To determine fair market value on a piece of art is difficult. It's worth what someone will pay. If it's from an established artist, there's a set price. Otherwise there's a discount. We just want to find someone who loves it.

"The artist sets the price and I will try to get market price, because that's where my commission is. If I'm dealing in higher end art or sculpture—$35,000—I usually have a wider margin to play with. I'd rather make 10 percent of something instead of 20 percent of nothing.

"It's up to me to know what I want out of the deal to make it work.

"I have to be able to justify, through past sales, the price of this work. The client needs to know they are paying fair market value—market being set by previous sales. If the client has a budget of $25,000, he can't buy one piece for $25,000 if he needs 10 pieces of art. If we can't find agreement, I will find something comparable, something with the same visual impact. I'll substitute what they first wanted for what they can really afford. I will get them something close. They either settle for that or they take the one piece they really wanted.

"In my work, I deal with personalities. I've learned how important it is to know who you are dealing with. You can't succeed unless you know your audience and how far you can tweak something."

The challenge of negotiating something that doesn't exist is making it seem tangible and valuable in the mind of the other party. That means creating a relationship with your potential buyer.

> "Youth is not a time of life, it is a state of mind. You are as old as your doubt, your fear, your despair. The way to keep young is to keep your faith young. Keep your self-confidence young. Keep your hope young."
> —Luella F. Phean, author

Zest for Living

Sherene Djafroodi is a dynamic young entrepreneur in her early 20s. She has an impressive track record of writing credits as a freelance magazine writer. Here's how she describes breaking into her profession:

"I mostly negotiate to get business. That means I negotiate cost, price, and ideas. I negotiate for the value of an intangible idea. I try to market my creative product at a higher level. I negotiate the content of the article with the editor.

"Along the way, I've learned that it is most important to always frame things as what you are giving instead of what you need to get.

"If I'm pitching a 3,000-word article and they only want a 1,500-word article, I will focus on talking about the original marketing tool that got them interested in the idea. I remind them why it is a hot topic and worth the extra space. I tell them why it's a good fit for their audience.

"It matters what kind of relationship I have with the editor, of course. If you're generating lots of good ideas, they want first right of refusal on all your stuff. The ideas and the money go hand in hand in this business. Great ideas and writers who consistently come up with them are worth more to the editors than the money.

"I broke into this business offering thinking. I was offering what I have. Then I saw that, no, that's not really true. It's more about who I am as a person, as a writer. I offered myself. I said, 'I have something to give you, and you are going to like it.' I used all I had, I put everything on the line. It's been good because my age is a very marketable thing right now. They want to sell to my age group.

"When I want an assignment, I send them three quarters of a page with the lead on it. I state why I'm the perfect person to write it. They know I will keep on querying that article until I sell it to someone. They know it might run at the same time. They ignore me if they don't want it. Sometimes, they call much later and say, 'We want it now!'

"Then I'm in a stronger negotiation position. Eventually, once I get into a continual relationship with someone, I can negotiate a column for a magazine. By the time I had my third piece published, one editor started asking me for more ideas and for a column. That makes the negotiations much easier.

"Now, suddenly, I'm negotiating hard for this column. But if they don't offer what I want, I will probably take it anyway. I wouldn't let them know that! But why not take it at the highest price? Then I'll have time to put a lot more work into it. I like the idea of a column.

"I'm a feminist. The advantages of being a female in a negotiation are, well, I guess it depends on who you are negotiating with. Being in your early 20s and being a female is really valuable in my business, because that's who the magazines target.

"I find that if you are negotiating with women, they will stereotype you in a mother-child role, sort of take you under their wing. That's an advantageous place. It's great when a more powerful woman is now interested in helping you.

"When negotiating with men, I believe they don't take me as seriously as they do other men. They don't think I'm qualified. That I'm too young or something. What I mean is that with men, the way you present yourself, is by being very clearly *not* available. You need to make it clear that this is an even trade, work for money. Nothing else.

"Men who come to negotiation with a beautiful young woman are worried that she will use these weapons against them, so they have more initial resistance. You must make it clear that this is win-win on a business level.

"From my personal experience, women will only be jealous if you do something to make them feel jealous, uncomfortable, or insecure. I've never had the problem. I love women and love interacting with them. My opinion has always been that you need to check your own behavior, there's something you're doing to close off women, or you are acting overtly special. Grotesque jealousy is triggered by bad behavior.

"The thing that makes women better negotiators is that they are empathetic. This helps create rapport. I see that quality in a lot of women. That's the beginning point, learning to use rapport. Use empathy to see where someone is coming from and what they want, and determine if you can give it to them. I think that's the biggest thing."

In Summary

Using all your skills, knowledge about the party, and by being aware of the advantages of the deal, paint tangible word pictures of the benefits any time you're selling something they can't see, touch, or taste.

Chapter 29

Negotiations
With Loved Ones

"The go-between wears out a thousand sandals."
—Japanese Proverb

Some negotiations are critically important and require skills in addition to those discussed so far. While the negotiation skills mentioned in all the preceding pages will work in all cases, they may not produce the long-term results you desire when the negotiation, for instance, is with your child, parent, or mate. In negotiations with loved ones, your goal is to keep harmony and trust in the relationship.

Negotiating With Your Child

Dr. Zeynep Biringen is one of the world's leading researchers on parent-child bonds. Her work is celebrated in the new book *Raising a Secure Child: Creating an Emotional Connection Between You and Your Child* (Perigee, 2004). I cannot recommend it highly enough. Dr. Biringen was kind enough to talk with me about the challenge of negotiating with our most beloved people—our children.

She said, "I believe in emotional availability. I think it is difficult to negotiate with your child if you don't have the emotional availability foundation. As parents, we must earn the right to negotiate with our children. If they negotiate with us and do what we want them to do, it's because we are emotionally available. Their way of responding to us should be a signal that we need to work at the level of the larger relationship.

"This is not to say all children can be negotiated with all the time. Kids will try to assert their independence at different ages, have their points of view, and want some conflict. It's good for them and normal.

"My daughter is headstrong. No level of emotional availability will make it easier. I don't want her to be subservient. But I know I am dealing with a temperament issue. It's who she is as a person.

"Sometimes our children tell us they need one thing and really need another. Parents need to backtrack and see if there are harmony or obedience issues. Moms and dads need to take a step back and look at the level of the relationship. If you can access the high level of emotional give-and-take that goes on in the family, then when your child starts a conflict, lowering your level of give-and-take makes them lose something they are very happy to share with you. I am not suggesting withdrawal of love, but the level of enthusiasm and play, and the give and take and the sharing of positive aspects and emotions, is very important to children.

"If you are a person who is generally not pleased with things, there isn't a lot of positive affect sharing going on with your child. Therefore the child doesn't know the positive signal from the noise of your discontent. They don't know what they should be doing. But if you are generally positive, sharing and playing a half hour a day or more, they know more. That's because they are on the same wavelength with you. Your child can sense when you lower that level of connection and respond to it.

"Children get more temperamental and more moody as they age. It comes down to the negotiation. If you enter the interaction with the eye to negotiate and get what you want, then what happens with teenagers or the strong-minded child is that they may not do what you want them to do. They need to assert their individuality.

"Identity development happens during the teen years. Part of this is finding your own individuality and separation beginning at this time. The way you do that is to resist every once in a while. Sometimes you realize you overstepped into their individuality, and then you say you're sorry. There are reasonable limits, of course.

"I believe as a parent I should provide lots of information. She wants to wash her hair and go outside. We live in the cold part of

Colorado. I might allow consequence discipline. As parents we don't want them to learn everything through experience, and it's a slow way to learn. Although there some things they will learn only through experience.

"So I've been providing information. I say to my daughter, 'If you do this, the consequences may be this. It's your choice.' Giving choices is very good, but as a parent you know that the choice they make may not lead to the best outcome.

"Giving them choices when you haven't got an emotionally available relationship underneath is a bad idea. Leaving you out of the loop might mean they suffer too much. If you have a connected relationship where there is a safe place for them to come to, and then you provide information about what can happen and still allow 'but it's your choice' situations, then the child is empowered to make a choice and know there's a haven if it's the wrong one. They get to exercise their separation and individuality, but you have still created a connection.

"I think of it in terms of providing information. About sex, HIV, pregnancy, drugs, smoking: they get wrong info from everyone. They take their information from all the wrong places. We want our children to benefit from our experience but we want to not be intrusive. We want to allow them to find out who they are, but still benefit from our experience. The ideal adolescence is really moving off and then moving back to the safety of the nest over and over. We want our children regularly coming home to recharge emotionally. At all ages, what you want to be moving away and moving back emotionally but the connection is always maintained.

"It becomes a vacuum for adolescents. If they are emotionally empty they won't want to come back to us. We, as parents, desperately want them to benefit from our experiences, learn from us. We want to give that. But in adolescence, it depends on the level of emotional availability created to that point. The time to build emotional availability is before adolescence, but it's never too late.

"One critical strategy is to spend a half hour every day playing with your child while they are young. Take the phone off the hook, don't allow distractions. Even with an older child, drive them around to after-school activities and talk/listen to them. Talking and listening even more are the best ways to play with an older child—show interest in what they are saying. Driving time can be play time with teens. You need the basis of positive time in order to negotiate.

"You don't want to keep them from individuating or becoming a new person. Things can change abruptly, one needs to pay attention. Get into conversations about the changes that are happening. My daughter will say things and then come back and say she's sorry. I tell her I'm glad she said she's sorry, but I really need to see it in action.

"I teach my child empathy, putting herself in someone else's shoes. I try to remind her that she needs to think about how she's treating other people.

"Children have their own levels of availability and unavailability, as we do. As parents, we are trying to get children to be more available to us. We want them to have a good connection with us. Isolate these things you want to work on. Use language that will help them understand a more textured way of viewing the world.

"When I say, 'Erin, it really hurts my feelings…,' I'm teaching her that I have feelings, too.

"Parents sometimes think they have to do something to be emotionally available. Often, all we need to do is be available. Emotional availability is a timeless principle that, once mastered, will last through the lifetime. You have to watch for what the child wants. If you're playing with a baby and the baby is looking away, it is being overstimulated. When picking up kids from school, some parents launch into a long questioning period. Parents can be too available, which means too intrusive. We need to work with the child's comfort level. We don't need to do anything elaborate. We should be working on being available when they are ready, and allowing space for reciprocation. Rather than demanding interaction, we need to get the experience of the child. We need to read the kids' emotional state. Back off if they are not in the mood to talk. Drop everything, if you can, when they are in the mood.

"It's similar to adult relationships. Pursuing too much often leads to too much stimulation. Allowed space, children will come to you.

"People being available at different times doesn't work so well. One solution might be to have a conversation. Provide information. Say, 'When we go home, we won't go out again tonight. I'd love to spend some time with you, but I'll be working on a project so I won't today. Do you remember things that have happened like this to *you* in the last week?' Children don't think like that by themselves. It shows them that they can control their emotions as well.

"We have to become emotionally well-regulated as adults. What I do, as a parent who is tired sometimes, is announce (in my mind, to myself) that *this is tough for me. I've have a bad day. I'm going to be short-fused.* Then I sometimes say it to Erin. I tell her I'm really having a bad day. 'I really treasure our time together and I really don't want to feel exhausted, but I do.' Use language to help them understand where you are coming from. We don't need to protect them totally from what we're feeling. Too much protection makes them wonder if we don't love them.

"You don't want to necessarily hide things. If it's easy enough to put on a happy face, do it. If you think that what's going on inside you is going to overflow, it's better to talk about it before it does. Include the kids in it and have open communication. They will rise to the challenge. Then reward them with hugs, kisses, and words of praise."

Negotiating With Men You Love or Might Like To

Men, too, like to be rewarded with hugs, kisses, and words of praise. If you throw in a good meal, and possibly some physical bonuses, you can pretty much create him in your image. Most women have figured this out by now.

But like Dr. Biringen said in the previous section about children, "It's similar to adult relationships. Pursuing too much too often leads to too much stimulation. Allow space for our children [or men] to come to us."

We've talked about negotiation, the importance of knowing what you want, clear questions, and so on. There's a word for women who pounce on their man with questions designed to drive him to her conclusion: nag. A "nag" technically is a beat-up old female horse far past her prime, like the kind that are used to pull carriages. "Nag" is a bad word, a terrible label, and something you can avoid and still get the results you want.

If you're a single girl, getting a man you like to do what you want isn't rocket science. The trick is to not let him know you like him as much or more than he likes you. Remember in Chapter 12 we talked all about *you?* You've got to be cool and confident in yourself in order to know what you want and get it from the world.

Remember:

> There's always one who kisses, and one who
> offers the cheek.
> —French proverb

Most men enjoy the chase and like to be kept guessing just a little bit. I spent 10 years married and have now spent 10 years single. My married male friends who complain about their wives say that they lost their special touch, their allure. It's not that he's seen her sick with the flu or giving birth. I think it is mostly that she's stopped caring about keeping him in a negotiation with her—a negotiation for love.

If you lose someone's attention during any negotiation, you lose the sale. This isn't a book on sex tricks, or where to buy cute little costumes, or weekend hideaways where you can slip away with your man. But if you've stopped finding ways to hook his interest, you can pretty much consider the negotiation over. The marriage doesn't end the deal, it begins it.

Of course, he has responsibility to amuse, entice, and lure you into a negotiation of love with him, too. But he's not reading this book. Unless you'd like to find yourself outside of the relationship you are inside now, it's a good idea to understand how the principles of negotiation apply to marriage, sex, dating, and men. You have to change to get him to change. "Laugh and the world laughs with you" has a flip side: love and the world loves with you. If you can honestly give all you have to your relationship and it still doesn't work for you, you'll at least have gotten clear on your options: put up or shut up or leave. In most cases I've observed, men really do want their relationships to work. They aren't as good at finding us as we are at attracting them. For anyone who doesn't know this because they've been in a relationship a long time, there are truck loads, bushel baskets, and piles of ugly, hopeless, homely, boring men cramming the dating services. They need someone to love them despite their paunches. We can always attract them. The converse isn't true. Your man, if he's anywhere near typical, needs the relationship with you at least as much as you need it with him! You're offering the cheek, honey. Just make sure he wants to kiss it.

Negotiation With the Men We Love: The Seven Wise Sisters Speak Out

The first principle: We live in a world overflowing with abundance.

There is an abundance of pretty women, an abundance of opportunities, an abundance of other people to talk to, hang out with, fall in love with, watch wrestling with, or whatever. Don't sell yourself short, and don't be too precious.

The second principle: Negotiation is creating a situation in which both parties feel their needs are being served.

Having been married and single, I can assure the wives of the world that as soon as you stop rewarding his efforts to contribute to the marriage in whatever way he does with the most basic items—food and sex—you are setting up even the most evolved man for a difficult path. Meeting his needs is your job. You go first, and let him respond or fail by meeting yours. If he doesn't, you have a whole new set of things to consider, but nagging won't bring you what you want.

The third principle: Successful negotiation usually requires creativity.

Men respond to creativity. Change the way you kiss him. Change what you wear. Be creative about seducing him. The reason there are so many jokes about men thinking with two parts of their body is because it's true. Even if he's the most conservative, upright Christian man you've ever known, you must keep him mentally, sexually, and emotionally engaged to continue happily in the negotiation of your relationship.

The fourth principle: Know what you want and what's possible.

If you've been reading women's magazines drooling over the pectorals of the boys featured there, or wishing for the hour-long orgasm, you may have to realize that the man you love might not be qualified to give you what you want. Men with limited sexual histories are not likely to suddenly act like men who've been around the block, and you should be worried if they do.

If you read Architectural Digest and resent living in your one-bedroom apartment, and your man for not making more money to get you out, you may have a difference between what you want and what's possible. News flash: If it's to be, it's up to you. Either change your goals, evaluate whether he's the right person in enough other ways to compensate, or change your actions to create a different reality for yourself or the two of you.

The fifth principle: Be prepared.

Do your homework. Do you have any idea how much work it is to raise even one child by yourself? Do you know how hard it is to find a man who has all the characteristics you love in the man you've got and none of the characteristics you hate in the one you've got? Do some research. The grass is never greener on the other side of the fence— any fence. It's an optical illusion.

The sixth principle: Bring and show your best and highest self

When's the last time you made an effort? When was the last time you made a special dinner, got dressed up, put the kids with a sitter, seduced him in the car, offered him a little something special, did something nice? You can put a love note in his pocket, you can make his favorite cake, get him tickets to his favorite event. If you cannot say you've been being your best and highest self much of the time you've been with this man, you can't honestly expect the negotiation to be satisfying.

The seventh principle: Stand by your product, service, or word.

Did you promise to be faithful? Did you tell him you love him? Did you agree to share household chores? Were you employed when you got together but stay home now? Are you living by the formal and informal terms of your agreement with this man? Maybe it's time to listen to his side for a change. Maybe it's time to negotiate for equal rights, equal pay, and equal contribution. If it is, have your facts and be prepared to walk. That's the only path that leads to pure negotiation.

🐜 🐜 🐜

"Men: you can't live with them and you can't live without them." Katherine Hepburn wondered if the genders were meant to live together, and if perhaps separate houses was the secret to success in matters of the heart.

I am an ardent feminist. I am a former minister's wife. I've seen and lived enough in relationships between the genders to know that if one side suddenly changes and gives more, the other side either splits or begins to give more *himself.*

Stand your ground if he's already professed his love for you. The negotiation's success is in your hands. You have the power of love—the power of the universe. Wield it wisely.

If he hasn't yet found himself besotted by you, negotiate by remembering Dr. Biringen's admonishment to give it some space. No one, married or not, likes to be crowded to death. Don't suffocate your love. Choose your goals for the relationship and work them systematically, logically, calmly. Remember, you can always leave (if that's what it comes down to). Your mom was right; there are plenty of fish in the sea.

> "Love is what is left in a relationship after all the selfishness has been removed."
> —Cullen Hightower,
> American salesman, sale trainer,
> and advice author

In Summary

Love negotiations are like any other. What you put into it is what you can get out of it. Negotiate from the basis of love and you will achieve your goals and the best possible outcome for all concerned.

CHAPTER 30

The Tide Principle

"Most people live and die with their music still
unplayed. They never dare to try."
—Mary Kay Ash, entrepreneur

I've lived in Malibu for seven years now. In my stay here, I've met a lot of surfers. At first glance, you'd think they are all kind of immature. Most of them work to surf, and live in pretty shabby conditions in the meantime. But the older surfers have built a real respect for the ocean, the sea life, the moon, the sun. It comes from spending hours on the board. Negotiation, life, and surfing are actually pretty closely related topics.

One surfer named Steve told me, "You're out on this board and the water is all around you. You know there are all sorts of fish and dolphins and animals swimming in the same water as you are. You're part of them, part of nature, part of the whole big cycle of the Earth.

"The waves start with storms, when wind is caused by different temperatures. We know when there's a big storm somewhere, in a while the waves will show up. Sometimes from thousands of miles away."

The surfers even have a calendar printed a year at a time that basically estimates how good the surf will be on a given day. On days when there is no surf, there is no traffic on Pacific Coast Highway as I drive to work. But just before dawn, on days there are "good" waves, the road is packed with people and surfboards. The surfers are like the turtles that live in the water who instinctively know just when and where to lay their eggs. The surfers are connected with the sea too.

"The other thing is, you realize this whole world is a lot bigger than you," my friend says. "If you miss one wave, there will be another in a few moments. In the overall scheme of things, you're just one person. Sure, you matter, you'll always matter. But every moment of your life, there's so much to love. I could sit out there for hours loving the ocean, waiting for a good wave, feeling the rocking of the smaller waves, watching the sea life, the people on the beach, the seagulls. It makes you realize that you're part of something way bigger than you.

"All of life is like the tides, you know. It comes in, it comes out. It's all going to be okay. You just got to ride the waves that come, and wait in between. Your wave will always show up if you give it time."

Isn't that the truth?

Good luck in all your negotiations.

> "I don't know what your destiny will be, but one thing I know: the only ones among you who will be really happy are those who will have sought and found how to serve."
> —Albert Schweitzer, author, researcher

Bibliography

Allen, Marc. *The Millionaire Course: A Visionary Plan for Creating the Life of Your Dreams.* Novato, Calif.: New World Library, 2003.

Beckwith, Harry. *Selling the Invisible: A Field Guide to Modern Marketing.* New York: Warner Books, 1997.

Brooks, Michael. *Instant Rapport.* New York: Warner Books, 1990.

Davis, Phyllis. *E2: Using the Power of Ethics and Etiquette in American Business.* Irvine, Calif.: Entrepreneur Media Inc., 2003.

Elgin, Suzette Hadin. *The Gentle Art of Verbal Self-Defense.* New York: Prentice Hall, 2000.

Emerick, John. *Be the Person You Want To Be Using the Power of NLP: Harness the Power of Neuro-Linguistic Programming to Reach Your Potential.* New York: Prima Lifestyles, 1997.

Evans, Gail. *Play Like a Man, Win Like a Woman: What Men Know About Success that Women Need to Learn.* West Palm Beach, Fla.: Broadway, 2001.

Fast, Julius. *Body Language.* New York: Pocket Books, 1998.

Florida, Richard. *The Rise of the Creative Class: How It's Transforming Work, Leisure, Community and Everyday Life.* New York: Basic Books, 2002.

Freund, James C. *Smart Negotiating: How To Make Good Deals in the Real World.* New York: Fireside, 1993

Gallagher, B.J. *Witty Words from Wise Woman.* Kansas City, Mo.: Andrews McMeel Publishing, 2001.

Graman, Marilyn, and Maureen Walsh. *The Female Power Within: A Guide to Living a Gentler, More Meaningful Life*. New York: Life Works Books, 2002.

Greene, Robert. *The 48 Laws of Power*. New York: Penguin, 2000.

Hansen, Mark Victor, and Robert Allen. *One Minute Millionaire: The Enlightened Way to Wealth*. New York: Harmony Books, 2002.

Joy, Nicki, and Susan Kane-Benson. *Selling Is a Woman's Game: 15 Powerful Reasons Why Women Can Outsell Men*. New York: Avon, 1994.

Lama, Dalai, with Howard Cutler. *The Art of Happiness*. New York: Penguin Putnam, 1998.

Lawfer, Manzie. *Why Customers Come Back: How to Create Lasting Customer Loyalty*. Franklin Lakes, NJ: Career Press, 2004.

Ledeen, Michael A. *Machiavelli on Leadership: Why Machiavelli's Iron Rules are as Timely and Important Today as Five Centuries Ago*. New York: St. Martin's Griffin, 2000.

Lerner-Robbins, Helene. *Our Power As Women: The Wisdom and Strategies of Highly Successful Women*. York Beach, Maine: Conari Press, 1996.

Lieberman, David J. *How To Get Anyone To Do Anything and Never Feel Powerless Again: With Psychological Secrets to Control and Influence Every Situation*. New York: St. Martin's Griffin, 2001.

Myers, Isabel Briggs, with Peter B. Myers. *Gifts Differing: Understanding Personality Type*. Palo Alto, Calif: Davies-Black Publishing, 1995.

Nelson, Dr. Gerald. *Good Discipline, Good Kids*. Avon, Mass.: Adams Media Corporation, 2000.

O'Gorman, Patricia. *Dancing Backwards In High Heels: How Women Master the Art of Resilience*. Minneapolis, Minn.: Hazelden Education, 1994.

Qubein, Nido. *Achieving Peak Performance*. High Point, N.C.: Executive Press, 1996.

Redstone, Sumner. *A Passion To Win*. New York: Simon & Schuster, 2001.

Ruiz, Don Miguel, with Janet Mills. *The Voice of Knowledge*. San Rafael, Cailf.: Amber-Allen Publishing, 2004

Ruiz, Don Miguel. *The Four Agreements: A Practical Guide to Personal Freedom*. San Rafael, Cailf.: Amber-Allen Publishing, 1997.

Runion, Meryl. *How to Use Power Phrases to Say What You Mean, Mean What You Say, and Get What You Want.* New York: McGraw-Hill, 2003.

Spence, Gerry. *How To Argue And Win Every Time: At Home, At Work, In Court, Everywhere, Everyday.* New York: St. Martin's Press, 1996.

Weaver, Rix. *The Wise Old Woman: A Study Of Active Imagination.* Boston, Mass.: Shambhala Publications, 1991.

Werth, Jacques, and Nicholas Ruben. *High Probability Selling: Re-Invents the Selling Process.* Dresher, Penn.: Abba Publishing Company, 1997.

White, Kate. *9 Secrets of Women Who Get Everything They Want.* New York: Harmony Books, 1998.

Zick, Bernard. *Negotiation* (tape series). Dallas, Tex.: Bernard Zick, 2003.

Each quotation in the text can found at one of the following Websites:

AllGreatQuotes.com

Brainyquote.com

Geocities.com

HomePokerGames.com

IndianChild.com

Ishipress.com

Motivational-inspirational-corner.com

Quotationspage.com

Quotationspage.com

quotedb.com

Quotegraden.com

Quoteland.com

ShadowFoot.com

ThinkExist.com

WorldofQuotes.com

Zaadz.com

Index

About the Author

In 1989, Wendy Keller began a microscopic company with $150 saved from grocery money, a borrowed computer, a toddler at her feet, and a new baby on the way. Today, that company—ForthWrite Literary Agency—has grown to become Keller Media, Inc., a leader in information creation and marketing.

Wendy has successfully negotiated more than 460 rights contracts for intellectual property, including books, screenplays, special sales, audio programs, speeches, television rights, and merchandise in many languages. Her work has created opportunities for success for hundreds of authors and speakers worldwide.

Keller Media, Inc. (*www.KellerMedia.com*) sells books to publishers, books speakers for engagements, and trains people to succeed in both.

Wendy is the author of 27 published books. She writes under four pseudonyms, mostly on topics of interest to women or children. Her 16th book created such media buzz that her work was featured more than 400 times on shows as diverse as *Dateline NBC* to *Politically Correct*, and in print from the *New York Times* to *Playboy*.

A portion of the funds raised from this book and the speaking and consulting engagements that come from it will be used to continue the philanthropic work dearest to Wendy's heart and illuminated at *www.LifePresent.org*.

Wendy and her daughter Sophia live in Malibu, California.

To make contact with Wendy Keller or any of the interesting, fascinating, smart people she has mentioned in this book, call toll-free 866-62WRITE or go to *www.KellerMedia.com.*

You can e-mail Wendy Keller at WendyK@KellerMedia.com.

Keller Media, Inc.
23852 West Pacific Coast Hwy
Suite 701
Malibu, CA 90265